Dedicated with infinite love to my god-daughter Casey and my sons Jake and James. You three are the magic in my life. Thanks to Jess for bringing our boys into the world and to Casey's mum Linda and grandparents Ron and Sally Clarke for asking me to be Casey's godfather.

Amazing sauces, butters, bases and preserves
that will transform your everyday cooking

The
MAGIC FRIDGE

ALEX MACKAY

Photography by Peter Knab
Illustration by Us Now

BLOOMSBURY

CONTENTS

Welcome to the Magic Fridge

Open the door to incredible possibilities and enormous fun. I'll show you how to save time on your everyday cooking by stocking your fridge occasionally. Being prepared makes cooking more enjoyable and inspiration more available. Your Magic Fridge will go beyond tasty recipes; in combination with my kitchen tips and tricks, it can transform the way you cook and eat.

The idea behind this book was sparked at my old cookery school, Le Baou d'Infer, in Provence. It started with a fridge: the one behind my demonstration area that I filled with fiercely flavoured ratatouille and bright green basil pistou, deeply savoury chicken broth, spicy chilli relish, pots of luxurious almond cream and tart lemon curd – preparations I could use to build a simple meal or turn a nice dish into a delicious one. The fridge became like a person to me: a partner who always had what I needed when I needed it most. The stocks, sauces, butters, bases and preserves were always there, ready to help me conjure up the most fantastic meals and puddings.

To eat well every day, you need to plan and prepare. In this book I've combined the restaurant tricks I learnt as a chef in everything from Michelin-starred kitchens to tiny cafés, with the practical realities I've picked up from twenty years of teaching home cooks and cooking for my family. In any restaurant, of any size, the most important thing is to be prepared for service. Being prepared makes it possible to serve beautiful food, and it's the same at home: while you juggle your jobs and families, your service is your mealtime. It's also the best opportunity to spend time together, in the kitchen and at the table.

No matter how many times you're told this, it's not easy to just 'throw a meal together' unless you're a chef or have ready access to expensive ingredients and tons of time. But if you fill your Magic Fridge (and Fantastic Freezer) with my simple prepare-ahead recipes and use my kitchen tricks, you'll have the starting point for an amazing array of stews, sauces, soups, bakes, pastas, pies, pizzas and puddings, even meatballs without meat, upside-down tarts and an almost instant crème brûlée.

I've chosen twenty savoury and sweet base recipes, from baked beans to chocolate mousse, that are tasty, useful and varied. I've kept a careful eye on preparations that can keep for a long time. Some will be ready for you in the fridge, others in the freezer. You'll need to be careful about what you store your base recipes in and how you store them; I'll talk about this in more detail on p.13 as well as in the individual recipes.

These base recipes are, in essence, convenience food. They are a way of making fast food personal, so instead of buying a jar of sauce or a pizza base, I'll show you how to make a lovely version of it yourself. It'll taste better and you'll know exactly what's in it. Good taste, goodness and a part of you.

Your Magic Fridge gives you a head start: it enables you to cook fresh food because you spend time when you have it, in order to save time in the kitchen when you need it. You'll enjoy the wholesome satisfaction of making food yourself and the naughty satisfaction you get from cheating with food you prepared earlier.

Preserve food. Create time. Enjoy cooking more. Eat better. Magic.

THE MAGIC FRIDGE USER'S GUIDE

The tips that follow will make the difference between cooking being fun or not. They make the process more pleasurable, so whatever happens, your food will taste better because you feel better.

Before you start

★ Organisation leads to enjoyment. Have a place for everything: this is the single most important thing I can tell you. Not being able to find what you need, when you need it, is a massive cause of frustration and the catalyst for most things that go wrong while you cook.

★ Start with a clear worktop. If you start in a mess, you'll cook in a mess and finish in a mess. If you give yourself clutter-free space, cooking becomes easier, quicker and more fun.

★ Read the recipe all the way through before you start.

★ Work from a tray. Get all the ingredients for your recipe measured and on this tray before you start cooking. Line your ingredients up in the order in which you will use them. Once you've used them, stack any dirty containers back on the tray so that you don't make a mess on your worktop.

★ Anything that I suggest to prepare by specifying it in the ingredient list, you should do before you start with the method. With vegetables like onions and carrots I will tell you the size to chop them to, and the weight - because the size of vegetables varies hugely, and this affects their cooking time and the taste of your food.

★ When you preheat your oven, put the racks in the right place first while they are cold rather than hot.

★ Use an electronic timer always, for everything, for any length of time. It takes pressure off you to remember, taking an important concern out of your mind so you can enjoy the next job more.

★ Rearrange your kitchen if you have to, but work next to your cooker so you can see what's happening on the heat in a glance.

★ If you are serving hot food, it'll always be better on hot plates - heat them in your oven or microwave.

★ Always have a full kettle just off the boil. It's a lot quicker than boiling water on your cooker, and you'll be surprised at how often you need it.

★ If you don't have a dishwasher or microwave, please try and find space for both – they make life in a domestic kitchen so much easier.

★ I've cooked and written most of these recipes to serve two people because it was the easiest number to multiply to four, six or eight or divide to one. I've used measuring spoons wherever possible for the same reason. On the whole my portions are on the large side. If you scale the recipes up or down, take into account the size of saucepans and frying pans as more or less food will need different-sized equipment. In many cases, you can cook the recipes in larger quantities, to give yourself a portable lunch or meal the next day. I worked hard to make as many desserts as possible for two people because I think two is an often-neglected number when it comes to sweet things.

★ The 'prep/cooking time' indicates how long to allow overall to make the recipe. (I appreciate I probably chop faster than you do, so the prep allocation is the time I've taken, plus a bit extra.) The 'active time' is the amount of time you can expect to spend actually doing something rather than waiting for things to cook or marinate.

★ I am often asked what accompaniments to serve on the side of my main courses so I'll say if you specifically need a side dish, or if you don't need one but it'd be nice, or if nothing is needed.

Seasoning

The easiest way to make the biggest difference to your everyday cooking is to constantly taste and season.

★ When I say 'season to taste', but I don't specify in the recipe method, I mean that you should use the salt/spice/sugar at the end of the ingredient list. In terms of quantity, the right amount of salt etc. is the amount that is right to your taste.

★ When you add seasoning to anything, don't assume, always taste, then if you need to season again, do so.

★ Season from a height so that you distribute the seasoning evenly. Season on both sides and all over the ingredient.

★ When I talk about seasoning with citrus juice, I am specific about the amount as the quantity of juice can vary enormously depending on the size of the citrus. For the purposes of shopping, the average is 3 tbsp per lemon and 4 tbsp per orange.

★ Dress and season salads in shallow dishes. This makes it easier to get the salads fully coated with the dressing without bruising them. It's also faster, more efficient and if there are bits as well as leaves in the salad they don't all fall to the bottom of the bowl.

Storage

For every base recipe in the book, I'll tell you how long it will keep for in the fridge or freezer. These timings are predicated on the base recipe being stored in very clean, airtight, preferably single-use-sized, sealed containers or jars, kept in ideal conditions in your fridge or freezer.

★ It's amazing how much longer a preparation will keep if you don't open it, so lots of small containers are better than one large one. Equally, with smaller containers you have a smaller opening at the top for the food to oxidise, as it is the airborne bacteria getting to the food that creates problems. Depending on which base recipe I'm making, I put clingfilm, directly touching the surface, or a coating of oil on top, as well as a lid. This belt and braces approach helps the curd, pistou, relish etc. to keep longer. Look at the individual recipes for any specific tips.

★ Sterilising might sound intimidating. It's not: just put your jars through the hot cycle in your dishwasher. If you don't have a dishwasher, stand the jars in a pan of water, bring it to the boil, boil for 10 minutes, then dry the jars in a low oven for 10 minutes. Do this just before you're going to use the jars so they don't have a chance to sit around. You can also put the base recipes in very clean plastic containers, which can be more practical – but plastic can't be sterilised. (Saying that, I have tested the pistou in plastic alongside glass and it kept for the same length of time.) I like to use containers that I can re-use as many times as possible.

★ Labelling your containers with the base recipe name and date makes them safer, and means that you can find things easily when you need them. I use masking tape, clearly marked with a permanent marker pen. Masking tape is much better than any sort of sticky label because you can peel the tape off easily and it doesn't leave a gluey residue or come off in bits in your dishwasher. Label your containers in the place that is most visible when you open your fridge or freezer so that you can see what they are at a glance. Write a list for your freezer to cross off and add to when you put things in or remove them.

★ When you make something with the intention to freeze it, then freeze it when it is as freshly prepared or cooked (and cooled if it is hot) as possible. Don't put it in the fridge first and say I'll do it tomorrow; whenever I do this, it's ages before I get around to freezing it. Don't freeze preparations partially finished – for example, freeze the pizza bases (p.160) rolled out and ready for the topping, not in balls.

★ I know that defrosting worries people, and I understand that. For some of the base recipes in this book, you need to take them out and defrost the night before, others you can defrost in your microwave.

★ The key things are to keep air away from the food, to keep everything very clean and not to touch the base recipes with your fingers. Once you have opened a container or jar, clean around the insides or put it into a clean jar then put a clean piece of clingfilm directly touching the surface. It'll keep much longer.

KIDS AND THE MAGIC FRIDGE

I'm a cook. So I'm a magician. I can beat a bowlful of gloop into a mountain of meringue. My sleight of hand transforms flour, yeast and water into a living dough that grows into pizza. Under my spell, batter flips through the air to become pancakes and if I combine fire, sweet crystals and a few minutes I can turn raspberries to jam.

Cooking from my Magic Fridge with my sons Jake and James has helped me learn though their eyes and taste-buds. Both have a recipe in this book and both were independent about wanting it to be a certain way with a certain combination of ingredients. From asking me to help them with everything, they now want to do it all themselves.

Like the base recipes in the Magic Fridge, learning to cook gives kids a springboard to fly from and the confidence to attempt new techniques. Cooking educates kids in so many ways beyond the kitchen: cookery is maths, science, art, languages, geography, discovery, social skills, safety, medicine, and the most practical of all life skills. Kids who cook can inspire other kids to cook and eat well. They can learn, show and share the dietary prevention rather than the medical cure for many modern illnesses.

The more closely kids can connect the food they eat with where it comes from, the more interested they will be in eating well and trying new tastes. There are different ways to introduce them to this idea, and a great one is to associate cooking with the transformational nature of magic. Look at the Jam chapter: go beyond a spread for bread, and the jam can become a pudding, a pie, an ice cream and the base for wobbly jelly. By teaching kids how versatile food can be, your Magic Fridge sparks their imagination and feeds their curiosity.

Help kids grow this curiosity and develop their senses while they cook: we have this magical ability to differentiate between things we see, taste, smell, feel or hear. Encourage kids to smell, taste and touch ingredients, to enjoy their different colours and shapes, to learn the sounds of frying, chopping and everything that makes up the music of a busy kitchen. If their connection to the kitchen is magic, and their curiosity is encouraged, there is no end to the pleasures that kids can discover through food.

Getting kids involved as often as possible will capture them and keep them interested in food. Be safe, but try not to worry, let them make mess and let them learn to tidy it up, try different dishes on different days from the same base recipe. Start the adventure when you shop, show them that opening a box of clingfilm-wrapped pizza isn't as exhilarating as feeling the dough bounce to life in their hands, that picking up a jar of pesto isn't as exciting as blasting the basil to green goo in a blender that looks like a rocket ship. Encourage them to see cooking's fantasy side, the way that ingredients, however plain, can become something beautiful to look at and wonderful to eat.

Cooking with kids from the Magic Fridge is all about the everyday. Involve them in every stage; to decide what to eat, to shop, feel and choose the ingredients, to measure, butter bread, peel potatoes, grate carrots, knead, blend, stir, whisk, wipe and set the table, to pick herbs, squeeze citrus, wash dishes, choose spices, sweep, wash mussels and get them to learn how to chop.

At the end of each recipe introduction I've written suggestions about how you can adjust the recipes for kids, but still be able to enjoy the full flavour yourself. I've also highlighted which recipes are suitable to purée, chop or freeze for babies and toddlers. (I'll let you know if there are any ingredients that need to be left out before you purée.) A stick blender with a detachable stick and a chopping bowl attachment is ideal for both chopping and purées.

The base recipes in the Magic Fridge can be the foundation for kids to learn a skill that, no matter what they do or where they are, will be useful every day of their lives. Every action in the kitchen can involve an element of inspiration. Spend time in the kitchen then sit down and eat the fruits of your work together.

Could anything be more rewarding, more important, more magical?

CHICKEN BROTH

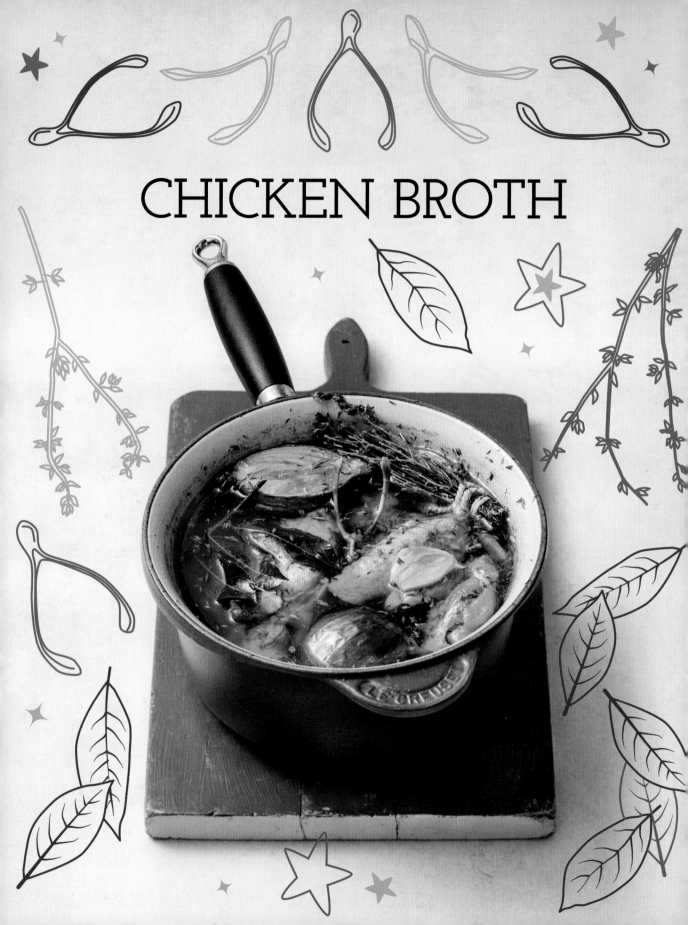

Chicken 'bone' broth is the trendy new name for chicken broth but whatever you want to call it, it is soul food and there are few things more comforting, restorative and versatile. I prefer onion, garlic, bay, thyme and peppercorns to be the aromatics in a simple broth, so that it stays neutral enough to be the base for a wide range of flavours. I'll only add carrots and celery if I want to taste one or the other, and you can make a good broth with just the bones, onions and water. It's a good idea to skim the surface, once it has boiled, before you add the bits and bobs: this way you don't end up scooping out a lot of what you put in. After that, you're only a gentle simmer away from a rich, clear, and oh so delicious broth.

If you have any chicken bones left from a roast chicken, use them to make broth in the same way. For a vegetarian and/or quicker version of the recipes, replace the chicken broth with a light miso or good-quality instant stock. If you don't have a big enough pot, just make this in two.

Makes Approx. 3 litres

Storage Fridge 5 days.
Freezer 3 months

Prep/cooking time 2¾ hours

Active time 15-20 mins

. . . .

3kg raw chicken bones
(or chicken wings)

3 medium onions
(150–175g each), halved

8 garlic cloves, halved

4 thyme sprigs

3 bay leaves

12 black peppercorns

1. Get a very large pot. Add the chicken bones. Cover the bones with just enough water to submerge them completely.

2. Bring to the boil. Skim off as much of the scum as you can. (A ladle is best for this.) Turn the heat to low.

3. Add the onions, garlic, thyme, bay leaves and peppercorns.

4. Simmer, uncovered, over a gentle heat for 2½ hours. (Chicken broth can be simmered in your oven at 100°C/Gas the lowest, which means you get less of the broth smell throughout your house.) Don't worry about skimming constantly, as long as you have taken off the scum in the first place. The fat on top enriches the chicken broth, but if you want to throw it away, do so when it's cold and has risen to the surface.

5. Strain the broth through a sieve into large heatproof containers. Throw away the bones, vegetables and aromatics. The broth can now be seasoned and eaten as is, used for one of the following recipes, left to cool and put in the fridge until needed, or frozen.

How to store

Refrigerate or freeze the broth in multiples of the quantities I use for the following recipes (750ml for the seaweed broth, 600ml for the pumpkin broth, etc.). I upcycle plastic yoghurt containers to freeze my broth in.

If you don't have much space, you can boil and reduce the chicken broth then freeze it in ice-cube trays. You need to do the maths first and label your cubes accordingly – if you reduce 1 litre of broth by 80 per cent to 200ml, then you will need to add 800ml water to return the broth to its original state.

CHICKEN BROTH
MAGIC IDEAS

It starts as a sparkling bowl of broth. The broth is plain, pure, hot and helps you digest and feel lighter. Chicken broth is a kitchen's great chameleon: you can change its colour with beetroot, its texture with butter, make it taste of the Far East with soy or let it sing of the French south with basil. In all cases the heat is vital. Broth is at its most satisfying when it's extremely hot, so heat your bowls before serving. You can do this in your oven or microwave, or fill the bowls with boiling water, which you drain out before filling them with broth.

MIX AND MATCH BIG-BOWL BROTHS To make broth into a complete meal you can add vegetables, proteins and carbohydrates. Here are 5 of each to get you started, then you can add to the lists depending on what you like or have in your fridge. Choose one from each category to cook swiftly in the broth.

Vegetables: mangetout, broccoli, spinach, peas, fresh corn kernels or baby corn

Protein: roast or smoked chicken, tofu, fresh or hot smoked fish, mussels, raw prawns

Carbohydrates: fresh noodles, dried noodles, ready-to-eat rice, ready-to-eat quinoa, pre-cooked lentils

Here are three examples of how you can mix and match by adding one vegetable, one protein and one carbohydrate to the broth. All the measures below are per person.

Broth with baby corn, prawns and quinoa: Bring 375ml broth to the boil, add 3 halved baby corn and bring back to the boil. Add 65g ready-to-eat quinoa (more if you're very hungry) and bring back to the boil. Add 4 halved prawns. Put a lid on. Take the pan off the heat and leave to sit for 3 minutes. Season to taste with salt and cayenne pepper.

Broth with smoked chicken, peas and noodles: Bring 375ml broth to the boil, add 100g fresh noodles and bring back to the boil. Add 60g peas and bring back to the boil. Add 80g shredded smoked chicken. Put a lid on. Take the pan off the heat and leave to sit for 3 minutes. Season with soy sauce and cayenne pepper.

Broth with hot smoked salmon, rice and spinach: Bring 375ml broth to the boil. Add 65g (more if you're very hungry) ready-to-eat rice and bring back to the boil. Add 50g spinach and bring back to the boil. Flake 80g hot smoked salmon or mackerel into the broth. Bring back to the boil. Take the pan off the heat. Season with salt, pepper and freshly grated orange zest.

CHICKEN BROTH WITH BASIL Make your chicken broth a vibrant green by adding 120g per serving of mixed peas, mangetout, broad beans, rocket and basil. To get the best and freshest flavour from your basil, stir it in right at the last minute. To make this combination even more special, stir in basil pistou (p.28) to taste in place of the basil.

CHICKEN BROTH WITH LEMON AND BUTTER I add lemon and butter when I want to both enrich the broth and liven it up: the combination feels very healing. Good things to add to the broth include proteins like hot smoked salmon or haddock, cooked chicken, mussels and prawns. I also add a green vegetable such as kale, broccoli, cauliflower or cavolo nero. To bulk it up a little, add quinoa, freekeh, spelt, rice, or small pasta like wholewheat giant couscous and macaroni.

Stir in 10g butter per 100ml broth at the end, with the broth just off the boil so that it emulsifies rather than becomes an oil slick across the top. Add lemon juice to taste. This is an excellent way to use the lemon butter (p.64), try 12g per 100ml.

CHICKEN BROTH WITH SOY, HONEY AND GINGER Add soy sauce, honey, peeled and grated ginger and chopped garlic to your chicken broth, a little of each to taste. I like this best with boiled mangetout and noodles and sometimes tofu cubes. Add lime and fresh coriander or mint for a fresh finish. For a speedy version use the soy & honey glaze (p.88).

CURRIED CHICKEN BROTH Add red curry paste (p.76) to taste.

Beetroot, kale, quinoa, seaweed & lime broth

Sometimes the idea for a recipe comes from the way something looks. I love seeing beetroot's vibrant purple seep into hot liquid, and this broth began there. I've starting eating more and more seaweed on the back of a tasting trip to Japan, and I've noticed with pleasure how it has become more common in the everyday culinary cupboard.

The wakame acts as a seasoning and what seems to be very little grows magically. The radish gives the broth crunch. You could add strips of the giant mouli radish, or if you have a spiraliser, mouli noodles.

I've served seaweed with noodles to my kids with great success. Sea farming and sea vegetables are going to be a sustainable part of the future, so it's as important to educate kids to eat these as it is to teach them how to use a computer. This is an excellent broth for kids, and it can be frozen.

Serves 2

Sides Nothing is needed

Prep/cooking time 15 mins

Active time 15 mins

. . . .

150g raw or cooked beetroot, grated

★ 750ml chicken broth (p.16) or miso broth

2 tbsp Thai fish sauce

4 tbsp soy sauce

2 tsp chia seeds

4g wakame seaweed

½ small mild red chilli, finely diced

50g kale, finely sliced

125g (½ pouch) ready-to-eat quinoa

40g radishes, thinly sliced

1 lime

1. Heat 2 serving bowls with the grated beetroot in them, either in your oven or microwave.

2. Get a medium-sized (20cm) shallow saucepan. Pour the broth into it. Add the fish sauce, soy sauce, chia seeds, seaweed and chilli. Bring to the boil over a high heat.

3. Add the kale. Bring back to the boil. Boil for 1 minute. Add the quinoa. Bring back to the boil. Boil for 30 seconds.

4. Ladle the broth and all the bits over the beetroot in your hot serving bowls. Scatter the radish over the top. Zest or grate the lime zest over everything. Cut the lime in half. Squeeze as much or as little juice as you like into your broth.

Buttery chicken, pumpkin, pasta & rocket broth

Pumpkin and soup will ever be entwined for me – it's a real classic in my native New Zealand, most commonly served as a thick purée. Here the chicken broth cooks into the pumpkin, giving it a deeply savoury quality and silky texture. I poach the chicken breast whole, rather than in little bits, to make sure that it cooks slowly and stays juicy. I like this with fusilli, but you can make it with macaroni, giant couscous, penne or orzo. Use quinoa or chickpeas if you are on a gluten-free diet.

This broth is excellent to spoon-feed as it is, to purée with some of the liquor, or chop and freeze for babies and toddlers.

Serves 2
Sides Nothing is needed
Prep/cooking time 35 mins
Active time 25 mins

....

★ 600ml chicken broth (p.16)

300–350g pumpkin or squash flesh (this is about ½ an average butternut squash)

1 skinless chicken breast, approx. 150g

100g fusilli pasta (or any other smallish pasta or grain you have handy)

35g rocket (½ average bag), thickly sliced

40g unsalted butter, diced

Salt and cayenne pepper

1. Preheat your oven to 50°C/Gas lowest, rack position middle shelf. Heat your bowls.

2. Get a medium-sized (20cm) shallow saucepan. Add the chicken broth and a pinch of cayenne pepper. Bring the broth to the boil.

3. Add the pumpkin and chicken. Turn the heat down to low then poach for 20 minutes, making sure that the broth never boils.

4. While the chicken and pumpkin poach, bring a large pot of salted water to the boil. Put a colander in your sink. Boil the fusilli as per the instructions on the pack. It needs to be just al dente as it will finish cooking in the broth.

5. Once it is cooked, drain the fusilli. Add it to the broth.

6. Lift the chicken breast out of the broth and put it on your chopping board. Let it rest for 2 minutes. Cut the rested chicken into 1cm dice.

7. Bring the broth to the boil. Add the rocket. Bring back to the boil. Add the chicken dice to the broth. Take the pan off the heat. Stir in the butter. Season to taste with salt and cayenne pepper.

8. Ladle the broth and goodies into your hot bowls.

Lightly spiced freekeh, soy, ginger & coriander broth

Serve this steaming wildly. Somehow the hotter the broth, the more refreshing it is, like a warm cloud engulfing your insides. It was while I worked on this recipe that I learnt to peel ginger with a teaspoon: simply scrape off the skin (it's much easier than any other way). I add the ginger in two parts - first to boil the flavour into the broth, then at the last minute for a reviving burst. The broth can be varied almost endlessly - I've made versions with prawns, chicken, pork, beef and tofu.

This broth is wonderful slurping fun for younger kids (and anyone who enjoys eating). Just be wary of the spice, so serve kids before you add the chilli and the ginger at the end. Use low-salt soy sauce and add a touch of honey if you're introducing kids to these flavours for the first time.

Serves 2

Sides Nothing is needed

Prep/cooking time 25 mins

Active time 20-25 minutes

. . . .

3 tbsp dark soy sauce

2 tsp peeled and grated fresh root ginger

2 garlic cloves, peeled and thinly sliced

★ 750ml chicken broth (p.16) or miso broth

½ bunch (4-5) spring onions

½ bunch (4-5) asparagus spears

100g edamame (soya beans) or peas

125g (½ pouch) ready-to-eat freekeh, spelt or lentils

½ mild red chilli, de-seeded and finely chopped

100g baby spinach

4 tbsp thickly sliced coriander

2 lime quarters, to serve on the side

1. Start with the broth. Get a large (24cm) saucepan. Add the soy sauce, 1 tsp of the ginger, all the garlic and the broth. Bring to the boil. Lower the heat to medium. Simmer for 2 minutes.

2. While the broth simmers, trim the roots and tips of the spring onions, and slice them thinly (1cm) on an angle. Trim the woody bottoms off the asparagus and slice the spears into 5 pieces on an angle.

3. Add the spring onions and asparagus to the broth. Cover the pan. Bring back to the boil. Take off the lid. Boil for 1 minute. Add the edamame and freekeh. Bring back to the boil. Boil for 1 minute.

4. Add the chilli, spinach, coriander and remaining 1 tsp ginger. Bring back to the boil, then simmer for about 1 minute, or just long enough to wilt the spinach.

5. Ladle the broth into bowls. Serve with the lime quarters.

Cook extra

Double the soy- and ginger-enhanced broth recipe above. Before you add the vegetables, pour half into a container to freeze for another time.

Prawn, orange, basil & bean broth

Inspiration for this recipe comes from the south of France. There is a legendary Provençal soup called soupe au pistou that I call on for the ballast of the beans and a burst of basil. The great bouillabaisse gave me the idea to transform the broth into an enchanting orange elixir with the scent and shells of the prawns. The combination of the two is blazing sunshine in a spoon.

I've learnt that kids often take a few goes to get used to the texture of prawns. Don't be discouraged if they don't like them at first. I was always delighted to eat their portions - and now they eat mine! This broth is excellent to spoon-feed as it is or purée with some of the liquor.

Serves 2

Sides Nothing is needed

Prep/cooking time
   20-30 mins

Active time 15-20 mins

. . . .

8 raw whole, head and shell
   on, tiger prawns

★ 750ml chicken broth (p.16)

1 tbsp tomato purée

60g mangetout, sliced into
   3 on an angle

1 x 400g tin haricot beans,
   drained

100g baby plum tomatoes,
   cut in half

4 tbsp sliced basil

Zest of ¼ orange

Salt and cayenne pepper
   or piment d'Espelette

1. Twist the heads off the tiger prawns. Take the shells off the tails. Cut the prawns in half through the middle, then take out and throw away the black intestine. Put the prawn flesh on a plate in the fridge.

2. Put the heads and shells into a medium-sized (20cm) pan. Pour the chicken broth over the top. Add the tomato purée. Bring to the boil.

3. Turn the heat down to its lowest setting and simmer for 10 minutes. Use a wire spider or skimmer to lift out the prawn shells, or strain them through a sieve into another pan. Throw the shells away.

4. Bring the broth to the boil. Add the mangetout and bring back to the boil. Boil for 30 seconds. Add the beans and tomatoes and bring back to the boil.

5. Add the prawns. Take the pan off the heat. Leave to poach for 2 minutes. (If you boil the broth after you've added the prawns, they will become tough.) Season to taste, I like to spice this up a bit with the cayenne.

6. Stir in the basil. Grate the orange zest over your broth at the table.

BASIL PISTOU

Pistou is the Provençal pesto. As parts of Provence have been parts of Italy at times, one is no more authentic than the other, and the ingredients are the same. I've adapted almost everything about the traditional technique anyway, so this pistou is truly authentic to me. My most recent innovation is to use the basil stalks: they have heaps of flavour and give you more yield per bunch than if you just use the leaves. My recipe is for the minimum that is sensible to make, but you can make much more - there is little extra work involved in making five or ten times the recipe. I've got tips for you on how to store it so you never need be without.

Makes Approx. 480g
(40 tbsp)

Storage Unopened, fridge
1 month. Opened, fridge
2-3 days

Prep/cooking time 15 mins

Active time 15 mins

. . . .

200g basil

6 garlic cloves, peeled and
finely sliced

12 tbsp (180ml) extra virgin
olive oil, plus extra if
needed and for the top

10 heaped tbsp (90g)
pine nuts

90g freshly grated Parmesan
cheese

Salt and freshly ground
black pepper

1. Get a large (24cm) saucepan. Fill it with water. Add salt. Bring to the boil. Fill a large bowl with cold water then put it next to your cooker. Put a colander in your sink.

2. Trim and throw away the bottom 1cm of the basil stalks where they will be brown. Separate the stalks from the leaves. Cut the thickest of the basil stalks as thinly as possible.

3. Add the basil stalks and garlic to the boiling water. Boil for 1 minute. Add the basil leaves. Push the leaves into the water to submerge them. Count to 30. Quickly drain the basil and garlic in your colander or sieve. Transfer them to the cold water. As soon as the basil and garlic are cold, drain them in your colander. Shake away any excess water.

4. Get your liquidiser. Your pistou will be greener and taste fresher from a liquidiser. A food processor tends to bruise the basil more.

5. Put the basil, garlic, extra virgin olive oil, pine nuts and the Parmesan into the liquidiser. Blend to a paste for 1-2 minutes. If the liquidiser blades turn but the pistou doesn't, tap the side to release the trapped air at the bottom and it will carry on. Add more olive oil, 1 tbsp at a time, if the pistou is too thick. I like a smooth texture, just short of a purée. Season to taste with salt and freshly ground black pepper.

How to store

Store in clean, preferably sterilised jars, of the size that you are most likely to use up in one go. Fill the jars up to 2cm from the top. Pour over a layer of extra virgin olive oil to seal the top: this stops the air getting to the pistou and is vital. Cover the jars tightly with clingfilm first, then with a lid. Store in the fridge.

Once a jar is open, use it within 2-3 days (or longer if you're careful and always use a very clean spoon) and cover with oil after each use. You can use the oil on top to make a salad dressing.

BASIL PISTOU
MAGIC IDEAS

To my taste – and after 29 years of professional and extensive eating – there is no savoury ingredient or preparation that will not be enhanced by my beloved, bright, beautiful basil pistou.

PISTOU-GLAZED VEGETABLES Pistou lights up the flavours of boiled or steamed vegetables. The amount you add will vary: try to strike a balance between the vegetable's natural flavour and the pistou. Make sure the vegetables are thoroughly drained and returned to the hot pan before you add the pistou. Try turnips, spring cabbage, leeks, carrots, beetroot, peas, mangetout, runner beans, broad beans, French beans, broccoli, cauliflower and asparagus.

PISTOU AND GRAIN 'RISOTTO' I cook dishes with a creamy risotto-type texture using quinoa, freekeh, spelt and wholewheat giant couscous. Cook them from dry, or use ready-to-eat grains from pouches that heat through quickly in stock or water. I fold pistou into the grains once they are hot to make them creamy and give them a vibrant flavour and colour. The amount of pistou I add depends on the grain I use: add it to taste.

GRAIN AND PISTOU SALAD Pistou is an excellent salad dressing for cold grains. Stir pistou into cooked grains to taste and you have a salad to eat as is or a base for cooked and raw vegetables. Camargue red rice with pistou, halved baby plum tomatoes and chopped sundried tomatoes is a particular favourite.

PISTOU DIPS Pistou is a dip on its own, or you can mix it with puréed chickpeas or chestnut purée to get a similar texture to hummus. Try a great variety of crisp vegetables. Baby gem lettuce and chicory leaves make perfect scoops for dips. Try whole Chantenay carrots, radishes with their leaves on, cherry tomatoes, fennel, raw broccoli, cauliflower and bouquets of watercress. The combination of these vegetables in their natural shapes and bright green pistou is one of the prettiest compositions you'll ever see. Chickpea or chestnut 'pistou hummus' also makes a great side dish for fish, lamb or roast aubergine.

PISTOU PASTA Stir 5 tbsp pistou into each 100g (weight before boiling) of pasta when it is cooked. Fusilli is my favourite because the pistou gets caught in the pasta's grooves rather than slipping through as it does with spaghetti. Add 2-4 tbsp of the pasta's cooking water to make the pasta and pistou creamier.

CRISP PISTOU SALAD Toss pistou with crisp baby gem or romaine leaves and spicy watercress or rocket, freshly grated lemon zest, lemon juice, black pepper and salt flakes.

PISTOU EGGS Whisk pistou into eggs before you scramble them or make them into omelettes. 1 tbsp of pistou per egg works well for me.

PISTOU BARBECUE OR GRILL I add just enough extra olive oil to make my pistou more liquid so I can brush a thin layer over grilled ingredients once they're cooked. This gives me the ingredients' clean grilled taste and the basil pistou's fresh flavour. Good seafood to grill with pistou: mussels, salmon, sardines or mackerel. Meat: beef, lamb, chicken, chorizo. Vegetables: peppers, aubergines, butternut squash, mushrooms and tomatoes. Cheese: halloumi.

PISTOU 'PITZAS' Spread pistou on pitta bread then top with one of the following combinations to make a quick pizza: Tomatoes, basil and mozzarella • Courgette and feta • Smoked salmon and mascarpone • Brie, bacon and sunblush tomatoes • Rocket, Roquefort and chorizo • Ham, tomato and Cheddar. Bake for 6-8 minutes at 230°C/Gas 8 or until the cheese is golden and the pitta crisp.

BAKED OR GRILLED PISTOU WRAPS This is ideal if you have a panini maker; if not they take longer in the oven but are still superb. Any of the above 'pitza' combinations work. Spread pistou over a wrap. Put the fillings over one side and fold it into a half-moon. Grill for 3-4 minutes or bake for 8-10 minutes at 180°C/Gas 4 or until it is all wonderfully melted and gooey inside.

PISTOU BAKED POTATO BRUNCH Spread pistou over a baked potato then top with cream cheese and smoked salmon, spinach and poached eggs, or Parma/Bayonne ham and fried eggs.

MOVE AROUND YOUR MAGIC FRIDGE Use your basil pistou to flavour broth (p.16), ratatouille (p.112), baked beans (p.100), pepper chutney (p.136) and cheese sauce (p.40). It is excellent spread onto the pizza bases (p.160)

Baked mushrooms with pistou, asparagus & fried eggs

Frying rather than poaching the eggs for this dish is part of my continuing evolution from chef to cook; unless an egg goes straight from warm hen to warm water, a poached runny yolk can be a complicated affair. When I worked at 2-star-Michelin Jean Bardet in Tours, we'd poach more than 150 guinea fowl eggs a day and serve them with white asparagus. The memory of all those eggs led me to this dish and then the pistou came along to make the whole thing sing louder.

Serve the tops of asparagus to the kids as soldiers to dip into the yolks. The tough skins on the lower halves of asparagus spears tend to put younger kids off, so it's best to peel them. Kids can find the slimy texture of mushrooms a lot to deal with, so chop them up and mix with the diced bread to introduce their texture gradually. This is good to purée or chop and freeze for babies and toddlers.

Serves 2

Sides Nothing is needed

Prep/cooking time 30-35 mins

Active time 20-25 mins

. . . .

½ baguette

3 tbsp extra virgin olive oil, plus extra for frying the eggs

4 large flat mushrooms (these are sold by weight in 250g packs in supermarkets, look for a pack that holds 4, not 3)

1 bunch (10-14 spears) asparagus, woody ends trimmed off

4 tbsp basil pistou (p.28)

2-4 large eggs, depending on how hungry you are

Salt and freshly ground black pepper

1. Preheat your oven to 200°C/Gas 6, rack position upper middle shelf. Boil your kettle.

2. Cut 4 very long thin croûtons from the full length of the baguette; chop the remainder into 1cm dice.

3. Brush each long croûton with extra virgin olive oil on both sides. Mix the remaining oil with the bread cubes.

4. Put the mushrooms, rounded side down, onto a baking tray. Prick them with a fork. Season with salt and pepper. Stuff the mushrooms with the diced bread. Push the mushrooms towards the back of the tray then put the long croûtons on the front.

5. Put the tray into the preheated oven with the mushrooms closest to the back, then bake for 12 minutes. Take the long croûtons out after 8-10 minutes, once they are golden brown.

6. While the mushrooms bake, bring a large pot of salted water to the boil for the asparagus. Once the mushrooms are nearly ready, boil the asparagus for 3-5 minutes until tender. Drain the asparagus well.

7. Put the asparagus onto the tray with the mushrooms and put the long croûtons back on. Spoon 1 tsp pistou into each mushroom. Spread a little over each long croûton, and put 1 tbsp onto the asparagus - make sure the spears are well coated.

8. When everything else is ready, fry your eggs. Warm a small (16-18cm) non-stick frying pan with some olive oil. Break the eggs into the pan. Gently fry the eggs for 1½-2 minutes until the white is just set and the yolk is still very runny.

9. Put the mushrooms, asparagus, eggs and the long croûtons on your plates. Trickle the rest of the pistou over the top.

Braised sea bream with spelt & pistou broth

Spelt is known as the 'caviar of cereals' in Haute Provence, and gilt-head sea bream as 'daurade royale' on the Côte d'Azur. This very grand sounding but economical couple combine to make a fresh and feisty springtime meal based on the glorious soupe au pistou of my beloved Provence. You can vary the fish, and add mussels or clams to the broth; you can also leave out the fish altogether, add more spelt or other grains and have a veggie version.

This broth is a lovely way to introduce young kids to new vegetables and grains. Good to purée or chop and freeze for babies and toddlers. You can also strain the broth and give it to them to drink on its own.

Serves 2

Sides Nothing is needed

Prep/cooking time
20–30 mins

Active time 20–30 mins

. . . .

½ large red pepper, halved, de-seeded and cut into 2–3cm dice

1 medium-sized onion (150–175g), peeled and cut into 2–3cm dice

2 garlic cloves, peeled and finely sliced

3 tbsp extra virgin olive oil

400ml water

125g (½ pouch) ready-to-eat spelt, barley or freekeh

2 farmed gilt-head sea bream or sea bass fillets, skin on

6 asparagus spears, bottom halves thinly sliced

50g podded broad beans (frozen are fine)

1 ripe plum tomato, cut into 1cm dice

★ 4 tbsp basil pistou (p.28)

Salt and cayenne pepper

1. Preheat your oven to 190°C/Gas 5, rack position middle shelf. Boil your kettle.

2. Get a large (24–30cm) shallow, ovenproof pan. Add the red pepper, onion, garlic and 2 tbsp of the extra virgin olive oil. Cover the pan. Sweat the vegetables for 7–8 minutes over a medium heat, don't let them brown at all.

3. Add 400ml water from your kettle. Bring to the boil. Simmer for 3 minutes. Add the spelt and simmer for 2 minutes more. Make sure that there is just enough water to cover the vegetables, the mixture should be a little soupy. Add more water from your kettle if you need to. Season to taste with salt and cayenne pepper.

4. Brush each sea bream fillet with ½ tbsp extra virgin olive oil. Season the fillets with salt and cayenne pepper. Put them on top of the vegetable mixture. Braise in the preheated oven for 6 minutes or until the sea bream is barely cooked through. Turn off the oven, leave the door slightly ajar, and let the sea bream rest for 2–4 minutes.

5. While the sea bream braises, fill a large (24cm) saucepan with water from your kettle. Add salt, and bring back to the boil. Boil the asparagus and broad beans for 3–4 minutes or until tender. Drain into a colander.

6. Transfer the sea bream to plates. Mix the asparagus, broad beans and diced tomato with the spelt mixture. Bring to the boil. Stir in the pistou. Season to taste. Serve with the sea bream.

Mussel tagliatelle with pistou, cream & chilli

Mussels are nature's fast food. The sweet and salty juice stored in their shells make them self-seasoning, self-saucing and able to provide the stock for a soup. The simplest route to the table would be to boil the mussels open in 4 tbsp water, stir in the pistou then eat them with some baguette. But since I worked for Don Alfonso in St Agata (near Sorrento in Italy), who taught me how to cook shellfish with spaghetti, I've loved the way shellfish juice gets absorbed into pasta, so that's what I'm giving you here. You can replace the fresh pasta with dried and adjust the cooking time accordingly.

From the snare-drum sound they make when you wash them in a colander to the shells snapping open when they cook, mussels are magical entertainment for kids of all ages. Boil the mussels in a pan with a glass lid and encourage your kids to watch them open; this is incredibly exciting and partially why my kids love to eat mussels. Teach them to use an empty shell as a pair of tongs to pick the other mussels out.

Serves 2

Sides Nothing is needed

Prep/cooking time 15 mins

Active time 15 mins

....

1kg mussels

4 tbsp water

½ mild red chilli, de-seeded and finely chopped

300g fresh tagliatelle pasta

5 tbsp (75ml) double cream

★ 5 tbsp basil pistou (p.28)

1. Get a large (24cm) saucepan. Fill it with water. Add salt. Bring to the boil.

2. Meanwhile, prepare the mussels. Pull the hairy beards out of each mussel by pulling each one from the thin to the thick end of each shell. Put each mussel into a colander and throw away each beard as you go. Wash the mussels well, enjoying the sound they make. If any are open, tap them lightly: if they don't close by themselves then throw them away. I usually lose 2–3 mussels per kilo like this.

3. Get a large (24-26cm) sauté pan or saucepan that you have a lid for. Add the 4 tbsp water and the chopped chilli. Bring to the boil. Add the mussels. Put the colander back in the sink to drain the tagliatelle. Cover the pan. Bring to the boil over a high heat. Boil as fast as you can for 2–3 minutes or until all the mussels open. Throw out any that don't. Take the pan off the heat; the mussels can wait for the tagliatelle if you need them to.

4. While the mussels steam open, boil the tagliatelle for 3–4 minutes. Taste and be careful: you need to undercook the tagliatelle slightly because it turns to mush quickly. Drain.

5. Add the tagliatelle to the mussels. Add the cream. Bring to the boil and boil for 10 seconds. Add the pistou. Toss it into the mussels and tagliatelle, try not to stir too much or you'll break up the tagliatelle. Serve.

Fried lamb with pistou, apricots & caper dressing

Lamb and pistou are a natural pairing. If you want to try the simplest version, grill or fry the chops then smother them with pistou and you'll have a feast. This recipe calls on a little North African influence and would also be good with mackerel, chicken or roast butternut squash in place of the lamb.

Leave out a little of the spice then this is good to purée or chop and freeze for babies and toddlers.

Serves 2

Sides Grains like spelt, barley or freekeh work well with this

Prep/cooking time 20-25 mins

Active time 20 mins

. . . .

Grated zest of ½ lemon and 1 tbsp juice

Grated zest of ½ orange and 3 tbsp juice

½ tsp ground cumin

2 tsp peeled and grated fresh root ginger

6 ready-to-eat dried apricots, cut into 1cm dice

60g pomegranate seeds

1 tbsp small capers

1 tbsp vegetable oil

4-6 large lamb cutlets, depending on how hungry you are

4 heaped tbsp flaked almonds

100ml chicken stock or broth, fresh (p.16) or made with powder/cube/paste

★ 4 tbsp basil pistou (p.28)

Salt, ground cumin and caster sugar

1. Start with the dressing. Get a large bowl. Add the citrus zests and juices. Whisk in the cumin and the ginger. Add the apricots, pomegranate seeds and capers.

2. Next, put a plate next to your cooker. Get a medium to large (24-26cm) frying pan. Add the vegetable oil and get it very hot. While the oil heats, season the lamb cutlets with salt and cumin. Fry the cutlets over a high heat for 2 minutes on each side, or until they are dark golden brown. This cooks them just past medium rare. Transfer the lamb to the plate next to your cooker to rest while you finish everything else.

3. Add the almonds to the pan. Sauté for 30 seconds to a minute until they are pale gold. Season with salt and cumin. Tip them onto the plate next to the lamb.

4. Add the chicken stock to the pan. Boil to reduce it by half. Add the dressing to the pan. Bring to the boil. Turn off the heat. Stir in the pistou. Season to taste with salt, cumin and sugar.

5. Put the lamb cutlets onto plates. Spoon the dressing over them. Sprinkle the almonds over the top.

CHEESE SAUCE

I can't resist a dish that oozes cheese sauce. As I write my mouth waters at the memory of eating little buns in New Orleans. They were warm from the oven and crayfish in hot cheese sauce burst from every bite. Cheese sauce is all rich goodness and flavour, and there is something wonderfully childish about it. Speaking of childhood, you may have memories of lumps; let's leave them in the past with my stress-free technique. The lumps are all dealt with before the sauce starts to cook, and so long as you keep stirring while the sauce comes to the boil and for 1 minute when it does, the result is silky, the taste free of flour and the cooking a pleasure.

Cheese sauce tastes better when it's cooked with organic full-cream milk. It has all the goodness I remember from the creamy topped bottles of my childhood.

Makes Approx. 840ml (feel free to make more), for a spoon-coating texture

Storage Fridge 3–5 days. Freezer 3 months

Prep/cooking time 15 mins

Active time 15 mins

. . . .

50g unsalted butter

50g plain flour

570ml organic full-cream milk

220g mature Cheddar or Gruyère cheese, grated

Salt and freshly ground black pepper

1. Start by getting the very clean, plastic containers that you are going to store the cheese sauce in ready. It's best to fill them while the sauce is still hot. I freeze the sauce in weights that are the multiples of the recipes that I will use it for. The following recipes use the sauce in multiples of 120g.

2. Get a medium-sized (20cm) saucepan. Add the butter. Melt the butter over a medium heat.

3. Take the pan off the heat. Whisk in the flour. Add the milk then whisk until the mixture is completely smooth.

4. Put the pan back over a medium heat. Bring the sauce to the boil slowly, whisking all the time. Boil for 1 minute. Be sure you get your whisk all over the base and into the corners of the pan as the sauce boils, so that it doesn't catch on the bottom of the pan. Take the pan off the heat.

5. Add the grated cheese and stir until it has melted. Season with salt and freshly ground black pepper.

How to store

Store in your containers. Cover the sauce with clingfilm, pushing it down to directly touch the surface of the sauce to stop a skin forming on top. Leave to cool then seal the containers with a preferably airtight lid. Store in your fridge or freezer.

When you need to warm the sauce to use it for other recipes, the best way I have found is in the microwave. Warm through a bit, then stir out the lumps, then warm a little more if you need to. If you don't have a microwave, warm it very slowly in a stainless-steel pan. When you defrost cheese sauce, it tends to look as if it has separated. Don't worry, just whisk it thoroughly and it is as good as new again.

CHEESE SAUCE
MAGIC IDEAS

There is no other sauce to which so many dishes owe so much. You'll find cheese sauce in the tastiest of places; on golden gratins, Greek moussaka, Italian lasagne, French soufflés, English pies, American bakes and even over a rare bit of toast from Wales.

CHANGE-THE-CHEESE SAUCE The first thing you can do to transform your cheese sauce is to change the cheese. The cheese can depend entirely on whatever tickles your fancy, whatever you have in the fridge and whatever you are most likely to use the sauce for. I generally make it with mature Cheddar which enhances most ingredients without overpowering them. Blue cheese adds plenty of bite, and is glorious with cauliflower, broccoli and Romanesco. Parmesan adds a feisty note (don't bother grating Parmesan, blend it in your food processor) and Gruyère a fondue-like texture. You can also make a remarkable cheese sauce with the whizzed-up remnants of a cheese-board! Mild cheeses are too timid to make any impact.

THE ULTIMATE CAULIFLOWER CHEESE Along with the sauce, two things make great cauliflower cheese. One, using the ribs and leaves (which account for one-third of the cauliflower's weight): this brightens up the bake and adds layers of taste and texture. Two, drying the cooked cauliflower in a colander in the oven, then seasoning it before mixing in the sauce: this makes the cauliflower taste more intensely of itself and removes excess water that would dilute the sauce.

Boil the cauliflower ribs for 2 minutes, add the florets and greens. Boil for 4–5 minutes or until tender. Drain in a metal colander. Dry in your oven at 190°C/Gas 5 for 10 minutes. Put the cauliflower into a baking dish and season. Gently fold 600g warm cheese sauce through the cauliflower. Sprinkle 100g grated Cheddar over the top. Bake for 25–30 minutes at 190°C/Gas 5 until bubbling and golden, or heat in the microwave on medium for 4–5 minutes then grill for 2–3 minutes until golden.

Variations: Replace the cauliflower with one or a mixture of steamed broccoli, spinach or Swiss chard. For extra depth of flavour add sautéed bacon lardons, reconstituted dried porcini, caramelised onions or chopped rosemary.

MUSSEL AND POTATO CHEESY BAKE
Per person, simmer 150g salad potatoes, cut into 1.5cm slices, until tender then drain. Boil open 18 mussels per person in a covered pan with 2 tbsp water. Take the mussel flesh from their shells. Mix with the potatoes, 120g hot cheese sauce and 2 tbsp chopped parsley in an ovenproof dish. Sprinkle 25g breadcrumbs over the top. Bake at 200°C/Gas 6 for 10 minutes.

Variations: Replace the mussels with poached smoked haddock, flaked hot smoked salmon, smoked mackerel or cooked prawns. Add chopped garlic and/or anchovy for a more intense flavour.

PUMPKIN, PUY LENTIL AND ALMOND CHEESY BAKE
Per person, simmer 150g peeled pumpkin flesh, cut into 3cm dice, for 12-15 minutes until tender then drain. Combine with 60g cooked Puy lentils, 1 tbsp sliced sage and 120g cheese sauce. Season with salt and curry powder. Spread the mixture into an ovenproof dish. Mix 2 tbsp sliced almonds with 25g grated Gruyère. Sprinkle over the top. Bake for 15-20 minutes at 220°C/Gas 7 until golden.

Variations: Replace the pumpkin with Jerusalem artichokes, parsnips, butternut squash or celeriac.

MOVE AROUND YOUR MAGIC FRIDGE
Mix cheese sauce with baked beans (p.100) and bacon, and top with grated Cheddar to make a cheesy bake. Mix the cheese sauce with ratatouille (p.112) to use for a bake or the stuffing for a pizza pie (p.170). To make a crisp topping for any of the bakes, try mixing Provençal breadcrumbs (p.148) with grated cheese then scatter it over the top. Mix the cheese sauce with cooked vegetables and/or ham or bacon to roll inside pancakes (p.172).

Cheesy courgette 'moussaka'

As much as I love pasta, I've always liked the idea of replacing its layers in lasagne with vegetables – something that moussaka does brilliantly with aubergine. Here, I've used courgette, seasoned with ras-el-hanout, the wonderful Moroccan spice mix. Cultivated rocket can make a speedy and spicy hot vegetable as well as a salad: you can cook it in the same way as spinach, or indeed mix it with spinach. In this recipe, I slice and then bind the rocket with cheese sauce. You'll need a 20cm ovenproof dish or pan.

Kids can have great fun with this recipe, they could layer their own little 'moussakas' in small bowls, you could even have a go at making little lattices with the courgette strips. Ras-el-hanout is an excellent spice mix to introduce to kids, warm and fragrant without being too hot. This dish is good to purée or chop and freeze for babies and toddlers.

Serves 2-3 generously

Sides A crisp green salad

Prep/cooking time
  25-30 mins

Active time 15-20 mins

. . . .

3 medium-sized firm courgettes

1 tbsp extra virgin olive oil

1 x 250g pouch cooked Puy lentils (or 1 x 400g tin, drained)

½ x 400g tin chopped tomatoes in juice

2 garlic cloves, peeled and finely sliced

★ 240g cheese sauce (p.40)

60-70g rocket (1 average supermarket packet), finely sliced

60g baby plum tomatoes, halved

Salt and ras-el-hanout

1. Preheat your oven to 200°C/Gas 6, rack position upper middle shelf.

2. Start with the courgettes. Line a large baking tray with a re-usable non-stick mat. Cut each courgette in half lengthways. Put the courgette halves, cut-side down, onto your chopping board. Slice each half horizontally into 3. Lay the slices flat on the lined baking tray. Brush the slices with extra virgin olive oil. Season with salt and ras-el-hanout.

3. Bake the courgettes in your preheated oven for 10 minutes until they are barely cooked through and light brown on top.

4. While the courgettes bake, get a medium-sized bowl. Add the lentils, tomatoes and garlic. Stir together. Season to taste with salt and ras-el-hanout.

5. Get a second bowl. Add the cheese sauce and the rocket. Stir together.

6. Once the courgettes are ready, lay one-third of the slices across the bottom of your ovenproof dish. Spread the lentil mixture over the top. Put a second layer of courgettes over the lentils. Spread the rocket in cheese sauce over the top of the courgettes. Put the final layer of courgettes over the rocket cheese sauce. Scatter the halved baby plum tomatoes over the top.

7. Heat the whole thing in your microwave for 3-4 minutes on full heat until it is piping hot. (Or bake for 20-25 minutes in your oven at 200°C/Gas 6 if you don't have a microwave.)

Cook extra

The 'moussaka' freezes very well, with a slight discoloration of the courgette and rocket the only downside. Make double the recipe and freeze what you are not going to eat before the last step.

Croque madame

A cheese sandwich made with bread baked at home is the first food I remember. Years later, after nights out in Tours, France, I'd buy hot baguettes at dawn through the back window of a bakery next to my attic flat. I would eat one while I changed from my dancing gear to my whites before I sprinted to work. To this day, a sandwich with cheese, often tomato and/or ham and sometimes an egg, is the food that I crave when I need a culinary cuddle.

This croque, monsieurs et mesdames, is the ultimate version of a sandwich, and for a recipe to be the ultimate there have to be rules. The first rule is that the butter must cover both sides of both slices to ensure that the base becomes crunchy. The second rule is that the sauce must be spread right to the edge. Dry-cured ham is better than cooked ham, and the slowly fried egg is the crown that turns a crusty 'monsieur' into the softer 'madame'.

Croques are good with smoked salmon instead of ham, or sundried tomatoes for vegetarians.

Serves 2

Sides Nothing is needed

Prep/cooking time 25 mins

Active time 20 mins

. . . .

4 x 1.5cm thick, 15cm long slices *pain de campagne* or sourdough bread, cut on an angle

30g butter, plus 20g for frying the eggs

★ 120g cheese sauce (p.40)

1 tbsp Dijon mustard

40-50g (4 thin slices) Bayonne or Parma ham

80g Gruyère or Comté cheese, grated

2 large free-range eggs

Flaky salt and freshly ground black pepper

1. Preheat your oven to 200°C/Gas 6, rack position upper middle shelf.

2. Butter the bread on both sides, paying particular attention to the base that will sit on the tray in the oven.

3. Get a small bowl. Add the cheese sauce and mustard. Mix together.

4. Next, put 1 slice of ham on each piece of bread.

5. Spread a quarter of the cheese sauce on top of each slice of ham.

6. Sprinkle 20g grated cheese over the cheese sauce on each slice of bread.

7. Stack 2 pieces of bread - ham, sauce and grated cheese side up - on top of the other two.

8. Get a small baking tray. Put the croques on top. Bake for 10-12 minutes in your preheated oven until the cheese sauce is golden and bubbling over the top. The middle needs to be very hot and the base crisp and golden.

9. When the croques have baked for 8-10 minutes, get a small (16-18cm) non-stick frying pan. Add the 20g butter then heat until it has melted. Break the eggs into the pan, and fry over a low heat for 1½-2 minutes until the white is just set and the yolk is still very runny.

10. Serve the eggs on top of the croques. Sprinkle salt flakes over the eggs. Grind black pepper over the yolks. Serve.

Raymond Blanc's crêpes

I learnt this dish from Raymond Blanc who hails from the region of Franche Comté in eastern France. It's a region where the pig is regarded as a walking meal, and many dishes are smothered in local cream and cheese. RB's crêpes are delicious, creamy and oh so moreish. So be warned, however many you make, you will eat them all. I used to cook extra with the idea of eating some the next day, but they would disappear in a single sitting. You can leave out the ham and double the mushrooms for vegetarians.

There is definitely an advantage to having cheese sauce and pancakes in your armoury when you want to get kids to try new ingredients. From vegetables to prawns, they can all be introduced inside these crêpes. This is fine to chop up for toddlers, but not one to purée for babies.

Serves 2

Sides Crunchy lettuce with a Dijon mustard dressing

Prep/cooking time 30 mins

Active time 15 mins

. . . .

1 tbsp vegetable oil

125g button mushrooms, washed and cut into 1cm slices

125g cooked ham, diced, or bacon lardons

★ 240g cheese sauce (p.40)

4 thin pancakes (p.172), or you can use shop-bought

100ml double cream

75g Gruyère cheese, grated

Salt, freshly ground black pepper and freshly grated nutmeg

1. Preheat your oven to 200°C/Gas 6, rack position upper middle shelf.

2. Start with the mushrooms. Get a medium-sized (20cm) frying pan. Add the vegetable oil and get it really hot. Add the mushrooms in a single layer. Fry the mushrooms over a very high heat for 2 minutes or until golden. Take the pan off the heat.

3. Add the ham and the cheese sauce to the mushrooms. Stir together thoroughly. Season to taste with salt and freshly ground pepper.

4. Lay out the 4 pancakes. Cover the bottom third of each pancake with an even amount of mushroom, ham and cheese sauce mixture. Roll the pancakes up as tightly as possible. Put them in an ovenproof dish only just large enough to hold them. It needs to be a tight fit otherwise the cream and cheese will burn around the edges.

5. Pour over the double cream. Sprinkle the grated Gruyère over the crêpes and cream. Grate a little nutmeg and grind some pepper over the top.

6. Bake in your preheated oven for 15 minutes or until golden.

Stilton & surprise Camembert bake

This flavoursome luxury is an example of how high the aspirations for a cheese sauce can be. I've called it a bake rather than a soufflé because the mixture only rises gently but has the stamina to stay up longer. If blue cheese doesn't raise your temperature, try any strongly flavoured cheese you do like. Milder cheeses are no use as they don't pack enough power for their flavour to get through the egg whites.

I've found that a soufflé mixture like this is great for younger kids. You will need an ovenproof dish that is 23-25cm wide and 5-6cm deep.

Serves 4

Sides A very crisp green salad

Prep/cooking time 55 mins

Active time 30 mins

★ . . . .

360g cheese sauce (p.40)

150g Stilton cheese, crumbled

40g bread or cracker crumbs

30g chopped parsley

25g butter, softened

1 Camembert cheese, around 150g

4 large eggs

Salt, freshly ground black pepper and freshly grated nutmeg

1. Preheat your oven to 180°C/Gas 4, rack position middle shelf.

2. Get a large (24cm) shallow saucepan. Add the cheese sauce. Heat the sauce, stirring all the time, until it is just warm.

3. Add the crumbled Stilton and stir over a medium heat for a minute or two until it is melted. The sauce may look a little oily at this stage, that's fine, it will all come right when you add the egg yolks. Transfer the sauce to a large shallow bowl.

4. Get a small bowl. Add the breadcrumbs and parsley. Mix together.

5. Grease your ovenproof dish generously with soft butter. Sprinkle in the parsley breadcrumbs and roll them around until they all stick to the sides and bottom of the dish.

6. Cut the Camembert into 6 wedges and place each piece at an even interval around the dish.

7. Separate the eggs. Put the whites into a large bowl and stir the yolks into the Stilton mixture. Taste, it is vital that the sauce is very strongly flavoured so that the cheese and seasonings make their way through the egg white. Season with salt, freshly ground pepper and freshly grated nutmeg.

8. Before you start whisking the egg whites, make sure that your oven is at the right temperature and everything else is ready. Use an electric mixer to whisk the whites to firm peaks.

9. Use a rubber spatula to scoop a third of the whites into the Stilton mixture. Briskly fold them in. Scoop this mixture into the remaining egg whites and fold it in gently, just enough to combine the two mixtures. If you mix more than you need to, all you do is knock the air out of the egg whites.

10. Spread the Stilton mixture over the top of the Camembert. Bake in your preheated oven for 25-30 minutes until it is golden on top and creamy in the middle.

SALSA VERDE

Salsa verde has a very big bite. It livens up other ingredients and revives you in the process. I have absolute faith in the ability of good food to cheer people up, and tart sauces that make you pucker up do it for me. I've used the Italian name here because the sauce's ingredients vary from country to country. An English green sauce is a white sauce with parsley, and a French sauce verte is a mayonnaise with herbs. Both are traditionally served with boiled or poached meats and fish. This saucy salsa can be served with anything from salmon to steak.

This is the sort of sauce that I've heard people refer to as 'not kids' food' because, I suppose, of the capers and anchovies, but this became my son Jake's favourite new sauce from the whole book. You may want to temper the mustard and vinegar to give it a slightly less scalding bite, but maybe it's actually kids' food for grown-ups to enjoy.

Makes Approx. 600g
(50 tbsp)

Storage Unopened, fridge
1 month. Opened, fridge
2-3 days

Prep/cooking time
15-20 mins

Active time 15-20 mins

. . . .

100g parsley

100g basil

8 garlic cloves, peeled and
finely sliced

8 tbsp capers, squeezed dry
and chopped

16 anchovies

4 tbsp Dijon mustard

4 tbsp white wine vinegar

12 tbsp (180ml) extra virgin
olive oil, plus extra to cover
the tops of your jars

Freshly ground black pepper

1. Pick the herb leaves off their stalks. Finely slice the herb stalks. Put the stalks and the leaves into your liquidiser.

2. Add the other ingredients.

3. Blend to a purée. Add more extra virgin olive oil if the mixture becomes too thick to purée.

4. Season well with black pepper, you won't need any salt.

How to store

Store in clean, preferably sterilised jars, of the size that you are most likely to use up in one go. Fill the jars up to 2cm from the top. Pour over a layer of olive oil to seal the top: this stops the air getting to the salsa and is vital. Cover the jars tightly with clingfilm first, then with a lid. Store in the fridge.

Once a jar is open, use it within 2-3 days (or longer if you're careful and always use a very clean spoon) and cover with oil after each use. You can use the oil on top to make a salad dressing.

SALSA VERDE
MAGIC IDEAS

Salsa verde has such huge presence on a plate, such guts and glory, that a lot of what you serve with it just needs to be a vehicle to hold the salsa. The ingredients to accompany it either need to be mildly flavoured and content to be completely overpowered by salsa verde, or so powerfully flavoured so that they can compete with it for your attention.

SALSA VERDE WITH RAW FISH AND MEAT The salsa verde's salt and acidity makes it an excellent seasoning. I use salsa verde to enliven raw flesh at the last minute, to get the bite but keep the raw ingredient's texture and taste. All the raw preparations are good served with watercress dressed with lemon, extra virgin olive oil and black pepper.

SALMON CARPACCIO WITH SALSA VERDE Slice very fresh raw salmon as thinly as you can. Spread it in a single layer over your plates. Dot a little salsa verde over the top.

BEEF CARPACCIO WITH SALSA VERDE Slice raw beef fillet as thinly as you can. Put it between 2 layers of oiled clingfilm and flatten out with a rolling pin. Peel the top layer of clingfilm off then turn the beef onto a plate. Peel off the second layer of clingfilm. Serve with salsa verde.

CRISP VEGETABLE CARPACCIO WITH SALSA VERDE I have two favourite combinations here, and if you can get to a speciality vegetable supplier for multi-coloured vegetables, this is the time to do it for the sheer beauty of presentation. The first is savoury fennel and radish, the second is sweet beetroot and carrot. In both cases you slice the vegetables as finely as possible then put them into iced water for 15 minutes to crisp them up. Dry the vegetables extremely well. Toss them with lemon juice, extra virgin olive oil and salt flakes. Spread the vegetables over your plates. Dot salsa verde over the top. Eat immediately or the vegetables will lose their crispness.

BEEF TARTARE WITH SALSA VERDE Mix very finely chopped raw ribeye steak with salsa verde to taste then spice it up with cayenne pepper or piment d'Espelette. Serve with a raw egg yolk in the centre and hot chips.

RED PEPPER AND TOMATO TARTARE WITH SALSA VERDE Dice even amounts of de-seeded tomato and red pepper flesh. Stir in chopped rehydrated sundried tomatoes and salsa verde to taste.

AVOCADO, APPLE AND RADISH TARTARE WITH SALSA VERDE Mix 2 parts diced avocado with 1 part diced Granny Smith apple and 1 part diced radish. Bind very gently with salsa verde.

INSTANT SALSA TARTARE Mix salsa verde with mayonnaise to serve with boiled eggs, beetroot or potatoes, fried fish or squid, cold ham, tongue or roasted/poached chicken.

HUMMUS WITH SALSA VERDE To make a dip with a hummus-type texture, mix salsa verde with puréed chickpeas or chestnut purée.

BURGER WITH SALSA VERDE This is outrageously good. Spread mayo and then salsa verde over the buns and lettuce, then put your patty and extras on top. You can do a bread-free burger too, using slices of romaine heart in place of the buns.

SALSA VERDE COLESLAW Slice red cabbage. Grate pre-cooked beetroot and raw carrot. Mix with salsa verde and lime juice to taste. You can add mayo; I prefer it without. Eat with any grilled fish, meat, halloumi cheese, whole grains or with the burger above.

EGGS AND SALSA VERDE Add a spoonful to boiled, fried or poached eggs or to egg mayonnaise sandwiches. Salsa verde makes eggs sing.

POTATO SALAD WITH SALSA VERDE Halve 120g per person of salad potatoes with their skin on. Simmer them for 15-20 minutes until tender. Drain until very dry. Toss in a shallow serving dish with 2-3 tbsp salsa verde and white wine vinegar, fresh black pepper and salt to taste. Leave to sit for 30 minutes for the potatoes to absorb the flavours. Add mayonnaise or crème fraîche if you want it creamy, or extra virgin olive oil if not.

MOVE AROUND YOUR MAGIC FRIDGE Salsa verde and pepper chutney (p.136) work brilliantly in combination with creamy cheeses like mozzarella, burrata and fresh goat's cheese. Scatter enough rocket or watercress to cover a plate. Spoon the pepper chutney over the top, put the cheese on top of that, followed by a few dollops of the salsa verde.

La grande salsa verde

I've called this 'la grande salsa verde' in honour of the way that garlic mayonnaise is served in Provence as 'la grande aïoli'. The salsa goes with so many ingredients from chicken to eggs, octopus to prawns, pumpkin to parsnips, green beans to mozzarella, that this is more of a suggestion than a recipe. I particularly like salsa verde with potatoes and eggs, so I'd be happy to have those two, the sauce and an hour or so to sit and enjoy them. The vegetables and meat or fish can be hot or cold, it's entirely up to you.

I love serving food to share at the table. Passing food to people makes mealtimes much more interactive, which helps kids learn to share and take part. You can turn the different ingredients into conversation starters to make the sharing about ideas and experiences as well as food. Everything below is good to purée or chop and freeze for babies and toddlers.

Serves 2
Sides Nothing is needed
Prep/cooking time 30 mins
Active time 30 mins

. . . .

300g (8-ish) small salad potatoes, halved lengthways

120g Chantenay carrots, washed and halved lengthways if large

2 tbsp extra virgin olive oil

2 large eggs

8 tbsp salsa verde (p.52)

150-200g cooked beetroot, peeled and cut into wedges

6-8 radishes, with their leaves if possible

2 large ripe tomatoes, quartered

1 baby gem lettuce, cut into 6 wedges

Salt and freshly ground black pepper

1. Boil your kettle.

2. Start with the potatoes and carrots. Put them into a medium-sized (20cm) frying pan with their cut sides facing up. Cover the potatoes and carrots with enough water to submerge them, no more. Add the extra virgin olive oil and a pinch of salt. Put the lid on the pan. Bring to the boil. Lower the heat to medium. Simmer rapidly for 7-8 minutes until tender. Take the lid off. Turn the potatoes cut-side down.

3. Boil for 10-12 minutes until the liquid has almost all evaporated and coats the potatoes and carrots. Take the pan off the heat. Season to taste.

4. Get a small (16-18cm) saucepan. Fill it with boiling water from your kettle. Put the pan onto a high heat. Once the water boils, add the eggs. Lower the heat to medium. Simmer for 8 minutes and 45 seconds. Drain. Peel under running water, more to stop you burning your hands than to cool the eggs. Cut each egg in half.

5. Spoon the salsa verde into a pretty bowl. Put the bowl in the middle of a large plate. Arrange the vegetables and eggs around the bowl.

Roast cauliflower with orange, salsa verde & mozzarella

Cauliflower has burst back into bloom. It's gone from a forgotten vegetable to a glamorous chameleon. Recent incarnations include cauliflower couscous, cauliflower steak, whole roast cauliflower with pine needles and cauliflower pannacotta. These ideas were unimaginable when it was only deemed good for burying in a cheese sauce (which can be delicious). I love the cauliflower ribs, leaves and stalks too: the younger ones make marvellous salads and the elderly are excellent steamed or boiled. Cauliflowers of all ages, cooked in any way, love to be accompanied by salsa verde. If you're feeling flush, replace the mozzarella with burrata.

This is an excellent way to introduce cauliflower to younger kids, it looks like a crispy tree, and my son James thinks it tastes like cheese. Good to purée or chop and freeze for babies and toddlers.

Serves 2

Sides Quinoa or wholegrain bread would be lovely with this

Prep/cooking time 30 mins

Active time 30 mins

. . . .

1 small to medium cauliflower (mine weighed 600g)

40g unsalted butter

1 orange

★ 4 tbsp salsa verde (p.52)

1 x 250g mozzarella cheese, well drained and sliced (125g drained weight)

Salt, salt flakes and freshly ground black pepper

1. Fill and boil your kettle then start on the cauliflower. Take all the leaves off but leave the stalk whole. Keep the leaves to make the salad with later. Carefully cut the cauliflower down the middle.

2. Get a medium to large (20-24cm) shallow saucepan that you have a lid for. It needs to be just large enough to fit the cauliflower halves top to tail: too large and the butter will burn around the edges. Add the butter and let it melt over a medium heat. Season the cauliflower halves with salt. Add them, cut-face down, to the pan. Put the lid on. Turn the heat to low. Fry for 20 minutes, with the lid on: the cauliflower face fries while the rest of it steams. Keep an eye on the pan so that the butter and cauliflower don't burn: you want the cauli to be golden.

3. Fill a large (24cm) saucepan, or a steamer if you have one, with boiling water from your kettle.

4. Trim any brown off the edges of the cauliflower ribs and leaves. Slice the larger ribs into 1cm thick slices. Leave the smaller leaves whole. Once the cauliflower has fried for 15 minutes, boil or steam the stalks for 4-5 minutes until they are tender.

5. Get a small bowl, a grater and a sharp knife. Grate the orange zest into the bowl. Peel the orange in strips, being sure to get rid of all the white pith. Hold the orange over the bowl and cut out each segment of flesh between the white membranes. Squeeze the juice from the core that remains over the top of the segments.

6. Toss the warm cauliflower ribs and leaves with 1 tbsp salsa verde and the orange zest, juice and segments. Season to taste with salt and pepper. Serve with the mozzarella, fried cauliflower, cooking butter, the rest of the salsa verde and a few salt flakes.

Pan-fried salmon with salsa verde, beetroot & quick polenta

With drama, colour and crunch, this plate of food has a wonderful balance beneath the salsa's bite - crisp skin, soft salmon, sweet beetroot and bitter chicory. Salsa verde is particularly good with fish and sets off the salmon's fattiness beautifully.

Take out the raw chicory, and this dish is good to purée or chop and freeze for babies and toddlers.

Serves 2

Sides Nothing is needed

Prep/cooking time
   15-20 mins

Active time 15-20 mins

. . . .

2 tsp vegetable oil

2 x 150g salmon fillets,
   skin on

100g 1-minute polenta

1 garlic clove, peeled and
   finely chopped

200ml water

200ml milk

200g pre-cooked beetroot,
   peeled and cut into
   orange-segment-sized
   wedges

1 head red chicory (or baby
   gem), cut in half

4 tbsp salsa verde (p.52)

Salt and freshly ground
   black pepper

1. This recipe comes together very quickly so make sure you have everything ready next to your cooker before you start. Get a non-stick frying pan just large enough to hold the salmon fillets: too large and the oil will burn around the outside; too small and the salmon skin will steam rather than fry and not become crisp. Put the pan on a high heat. Spoon the oil into the pan and get it really hot.

2. Season the salmon fillets with salt. Put the salmon skin-side down into the pan. Turn the heat down to medium. Fry for 6-7 minutes until the skin is golden and crisp. You can go by sound and sight, you want to hear a bacon-sounding sizzle but you shouldn't see any smoke.

3. While the salmon fries, make the polenta. Get a small (16-18cm) saucepan. Add the 1-minute polenta, garlic, water and milk. Bring to the boil, whisking continuously, then boil for 1 minute, still whisking, over a medium heat. Take the pan off the heat. Season to taste with salt and black pepper.

4. After the salmon has fried for 6-7 minutes, turn it over. Add the beetroot wedges to the pan. Raise the heat to high. Fry for 1 minute. Put the salmon onto plates. Fry the beetroot for 1 minute more.

5. Serve the beetroot with the salmon, chicory, polenta and salsa verde.

Cook extra

This makes a super salad for a packed lunch. Flake the salmon into a cooked grain like red rice, freekeh or quinoa. Grate the leftover beetroot (it usually comes in packets of between 250-350g), and stir in salsa verde to taste.

Skirt steak, salsa verde, spring onions & spinach

Salsa verde is divine with meat that is well caramelised. I eat it with lamb shoulder steaks, pork liver and chops as well as beef. Skirt is the tasty steak called 'bavette' in France and many UK restaurants: it comes from the flap of meat that surrounds the belly. I prefer to cook the beef in one piece and then carve it, rather than starting with two steaks. Skirt becomes dry past a very pink medium so, if you like your steak more cooked, you'd be better off doing this with a ribeye and adjusting the cooking time accordingly.

Serves 2

Sides Chips, or any spuds

Prep/cooking time 25 mins

Active time 25 mins

. . . .

4 tbsp water

1 tbsp vegetable oil

400g skirt steak (preferably taken out of the fridge 30 minutes before you fry it)

30g butter, diced

6 spring onions, try to get the ones with the bulbous tops

180g baby spinach, washed and dried if necessary

4 tbsp salsa verde (p.52)

Salt and freshly ground black pepper

1. Get everything ready before you start frying. Put a bowl to pour the fat into, a plate with a rack over the top and a cup with the 4 tbsp water in it next to your cooker. Put a pan with a steamer insert on to boil, or you can use a microwave.

2. Get a medium (20cm) frying pan, just large enough to hold the steak comfortably but not have too much space around the outside. Add the vegetable oil and get it really hot.

3. Season the skirt on both sides with salt. Add the skirt to the pan. Fry for 2 minutes over a high heat. Don't worry if the pan smokes, it needs to be this hot. Turn the steak. Fry for another 2 minutes. Drain the fat. Turn the heat down to medium.

4. Add the butter to the steak pan. Fry for 2 more minutes on each side (for medium rare, add an extra minute for medium). The butter will go brown and smell nutty, but it must not burn. Adjust the heat as you fry, and use a heatproof brush to baste the steak as you go.

5. Take the pan off the heat. Put the steak on your resting rack. Put the resting rack over the top of the pan. Grind black pepper all over it. Rest the steak for at least 4 minutes and up to 8.

6. Meanwhile, steam or microwave the spring onions for 2 minutes. Add the spinach. Steam or microwave for 1 minute more.

7. Put the steak on your chopping board. Add the 4 tbsp water from the cup to the pan. Stir it in vigorously. Bring to the boil. Boil for 30 seconds until there is about 2 tbsp liquid left. Take the pan off the heat. Stir in 2 tbsp salsa verde.

8. Spread the remaining 2 tbsp salsa verde over the top of the steak. Slice the steak against the grain. This is vital, it'll be very tough otherwise. Serve with the spinach, spring onions and every last bit of juice in the pan.

LEMON BUTTER

We tend to associate butter with creamy richness, but this one is all about freshness: it bursts with lemon to light up salad dressings, fish, shellfish, grains, green vegetables and pasta.

It's difficult to get the lemon juice to combine with the butter when you try to mix it by hand. A food processor is the best tool even though it still takes a while. The butter keeps for a long time in the fridge, and you can freeze it, so it's worth doing plenty. This works with lime too, but orange and grapefruit are not concentrated enough.

Makes Approx. 650g (you always lose a little in the food processor)

Storage Fridge 3 weeks. Freezer 3 months

Prep/cooking time 15-20 mins

Active time 15-20 mins

· ·

Zest and juice (12 tbsp/180ml) of 4 lemons

500g unsalted butter, softened

1 tsp salt

1. First, set up your food processor. Finely grate the lemon zest directly into the bowl.

2. Add the butter. Squeeze the lemons then add 12 tbsp (180ml) juice to the butter. Add the salt.

3. Blend until the ingredients are well combined. Don't worry if it appears as if the juice won't combine with the butter, it will. But it'll take at least a few minutes.

4. Put a roll of clingfilm behind your chopping board so that the edge of the board holds the roll steady. Pull out enough clingfilm to cover your board. Scoop the lemon butter out of your food processor with a spatula. Spread it across the clingfilm in a rough line, 20cm long. Lift the edge of the clingfilm over the butter.

5. Roll the butter in the clingfilm, pulling it tight and smoothing the butter into a cylinder after each roll. Once you've rolled the butter about 4 times, cut the clingfilm. Twist the ends in opposite directions like a sweetie wrapper until you have a tight round log, about 15cm long.

How to store

The best way to refrigerate or freeze lemon butter is to first chill it in your fridge until it is very hard. Then, take the clingfilm off and throw it away. Cut the lemon butter into 25g slices. Next, put the slices into a sealed plastic box so that you can get a portion when you need it without having to hack into the log. Keep some in the fridge and some in the freezer.

LEMON BUTTER
MAGIC IDEAS

Lemon butter gives food a real zing and an exhilarating burst of freshness. So even if you do nothing else except use it to season and moisten the pork, chicken, lamb, fish, shellfish, vegetables, pasta or grains that you eat for dinner, it will light up your mealtime.

LEMON BUTTER VARIATIONS Most ingredients love lemon, so the list of flavours to combine with it is a long one. It's great to have a selection available, like a little butter shop in your fridge and freezer. You can make a few recipes of the basic lemon butter, separate part of it, then stir in any of the following flavours. The quantities can vary to best suit your taste: Sliced basil or parsley • Peeled and grated fresh ginger • Finely chopped or puréed salted anchovies or anchovies in oil • Finely chopped or puréed olives • Honey and grain mustard • Finely grated clementine zest and smoked paprika • Ras-el-hanout • Curry powder.

BUTTERY RICE AND GRAINS Lemon butter will bind and light up rice or grains like quinoa, freekeh and spelt. Dice the butter, then stir in 10g per 100g of the cooked grains. My favourite with lemon butter is Camargue red rice.

LEMONY SPUDS Gently simmer halved salad potatoes, drain, return to the pan, then add diced lemon butter. Toss until the butter is melted and the potatoes are well glazed. For a fresh version of mash to serve with fish or white meat, add lemon butter in place of the butter in your recipe.

LEMONY SMOKED SALMON SANDWICH Spread dark brown bread with lemon butter. Lay smoked salmon over the top.

LEMON-BUTTER-GLAZED GREEN VEGETABLES All green vegetables get a kick from lemon butter. Boil your green vegetables in a huge pan of salted water. Drain thoroughly and return them to the pan. Add diced lemon butter, turn up the heat to melt it and glaze the vegetables as completely and as quickly as possible. It's like serving them in sunshine.

GRILLED VEGETABLES, MEAT, HALLOUMI CHEESE OR FISH Melt the lemon butter then brush it over the top of the ingredients while they are hot.

LEMON-SHINED CARROTS Put 100g peeled and sliced carrots plus 12g lemon butter per person into a shallow pan. Barely cover them with water. Put a lid on but leave it slightly ajar. Simmer for 10 minutes or until the carrots are just tender. Take the lid off and boil until the liquid is emulsified with the butter, almost all evaporated, and the carrots are shiny.

SILKY SOUPS AND BROTHS This is a real magic trick. Stir lemon butter into puréed soups to make them lighter and richer at the same time: pumpkin soup and tomato soup are my two favourites to do this with. Stir the butter into broths like miso or chicken (p.16) to make their texture silky and their taste more vibrant.

GLOSSY GRAVIES There is a French term, *monter au beurre*, that means to thicken and shine a sauce by adding butter. This can also be done with lemon butter for some extra tang. The quantities I go by are 20g butter to 100ml gravy.

WARM DRESSINGS Because lemon butter adds bite, it can become a warm dressing for lettuce, vegetable and grain salads with or without meat. To make enough for 2 servings, boil 200ml orange juice until you end up with 4 tbsp. Stir in 50g lemon butter. Season with salt, sugar and cayenne pepper.

HOT LEMON-BUTTERED TOAST Spread lemon butter on hot toast then put marmalade or lemon curd on top.

ROAST FRUIT WITH LEMON BUTTER AND HONEY Use apricots, peaches, nectarines, plums or figs here. Cut the fruit in half. Take out and throw away the stones where necessary. Per 100g fruit, add 15g lemon butter and 15g honey. Roast for 10 minutes or more depending on the fruits' ripeness. Baste the fruit with the butter and honey occasionally as they roast until they are soft and caramelised.

LEMON-GLAZED FILO PASTRY Melt together even amounts of lemon butter and icing sugar. Brush it over filo pastry circles or rectangles. Bake for 5-7 minutes at 180°C/Gas 4 until glazed and golden, keeping careful watch that it doesn't burn. Serve with cream and berries.

Mussels with lemon butter, greens & noodles

This is a beautiful balance between sharp lemon, bright green vegetables and the salty sweetness of mussels. You can use a mixture of vegetables or just one but whatever you do, try kale with the mussels - the combination is a revelation. Mussels are one of my preferred sources of protein, from their sustainability to their beauty, taste, texture and the joy they are to wash and cook.

Get kids to help you with the mussels every step of the way. Tip them into the colander together and enjoy the drumming sound they make. Teach them to smell the sea on the shells. Mixing mussels, kids and imagination is an endless source of stimulation and fun.

Serves 2
Sides Nothing is needed
Prep/cooking time 20 mins
Active time 20 mins

. . . .

4 tbsp water

1kg mussels

75g lemon butter (p.64)

2 nests dried medium egg noodles, or 300g fresh

200g green vegetables (spring onions, broccoli, mangetout, spinach, kale or a mixture)

Salt

1. Get a large (24cm) saucepan. Fill it with water. Add salt. Bring to the boil. Put a colander in your sink.

2. Next, prepare the mussels. Pull the hairy beards out of the mussels by pulling each one from the thin to the thick end of each shell. Put each mussel into your colander and throw away each beard as you go. Wash the mussels well, enjoy the sound they make. If any are open, tap them lightly; if they don't close by themselves then throw them away. I usually lose 2-3 mussels per kilo like this.

3. Get a large (24-30cm) sauté pan or saucepan that you have a lid for. Add the 4 tbsp water. Bring to the boil. Add the mussels and the lemon butter; put the colander back in the sink to drain the noodles. Cover the pan. Bring to the boil over a high heat. Boil as fast as you can for 2-3 minutes or until all the mussels open. Throw away any that don't. Take the pan off the heat; the mussels can wait for the noodles if you need them to.

4. While the mussels steam open, boil the noodles for 2 minutes in the large pan of boiling water. (If you're using fresh noodles, add everything at the same time.) Add the vegetables. Boil for 2 minutes more. Drain the noodles and vegetables in the colander in your sink.

5. Add the noodles and vegetables to the mussels. Make sure the noodles absorb the lemon butter and mussel juice. Bring to the boil. Boil for 10 seconds. Serve.

Red mullet with citrus, chilli & lemon butter

Provençal food is often referred to as sunshine food, and the idea for my red mullet comes from the great Roger Vergé's former 3-star-Michelin restaurant in Mougins above Cannes. Red, orange and yellow colour this dish into a sunset and the lemon butter is my 'magic' sunshine. It thickens the juices and softens the tartness just enough to create joyful harmony between the ingredients. Red mullet is my favourite fish, but this sauce is also delicious with salmon, sardines and mackerel.

I fry the fish slowly on its skin side so that the skin has time to crisp before the flesh overcooks. Crisp skin is a great way to get kids started on fish. My boys refer to fish skin as 'the crispy' now, even when it's not, so master the technique and get them started early. Good to purée or chop and freeze for babies and toddlers.

Serves 2

Sides Red rice, small or giant couscous for bulk. Romaine, chicory or baby gem for crunch

Prep/cooking time 25 mins

Active time 25 mins

. . . .

200ml orange juice

½ mild fresh red chilli, de-seeded and chopped

1 orange

1 lemon

1 pink grapefruit

1 tbsp vegetable oil

4 red mullet fillets (or other fish as suggested above), about 250g in total

★ 50g lemon butter (p.64)

Salt, sugar and cayenne pepper or piment d'Espelette

1. Start with the sauce. Get a small (16-18cm) saucepan. Add the orange juice. Bring to the boil and boil to reduce over a medium to high heat by almost three-quarters. You will finish with 60ml (4 tbsp). Take the pan off the heat. Add the chopped chilli.

2. While the sauce reduces, prepare the citrus fruit. You only want half of each fruit here, but you may as well prepare the whole fruits, then save what you don't use to eat with ice cream or yoghurt. Get a small bowl and a sharp knife. Peel the orange, lemon and grapefruit in strips, being sure to get rid of all the white pith. Hold each fruit over the bowl and cut out each segment of flesh between the white membranes. Squeeze the juice from the core that remains over the top of the segments. Transfer half the segments to your chopping board and cut each one in three. (Put the rest of the segments in the fridge.)

3. Get a large (26-30cm) non-stick frying pan. If the pan is not non-stick, the red mullet will always stick. The skin is very delicate. Add the vegetable oil and get it really hot. Season the red mullet fillets with salt and cayenne pepper. Fry for 30 seconds on the flesh side. Turn the red mullet. Turn the heat to low. Fry the red mullet for 3 minutes on the skin side. Turn the heat up to medium if you stop hearing a sizzle.

4. While the red mullet fries, make the sauce. Bring the reduced orange juice to the boil. Turn the heat to low. Whisk the lemon butter into the juice. Make sure it doesn't boil again at this point or the sauce will separate. Take the pan off the heat. Add the citrus segments and shake rather than stir to combine them, otherwise you will break the segments up. Season to taste with salt and enough sugar to balance the acidity. Spoon the sauce onto plates. Use a fish slice to put the red mullet on top with its skin facing up.

Chicken leg roast'n'braise with peppers, onions & lemon butter

I developed my 'roast'n'braise' technique for my last book, Everybody Everyday, to get the best from two cooking methods: roasting and braising. When you braise chicken legs in a covered pot or pan you get soft meat and vegetables but no roasted flavour; if you roast everything, you miss out in the lovely sauciness you get when you braise. To solve this, my roast'n'braise technique roasts the chicken on top of a foil-sealed frying pan, while the vegetables braise underneath the foil. I then remove the foil so the chicken and vegetables can become a harmonious stew, and the lemon butter lifts everything it touches.

I've learnt that kids love eating chicken off the bone, and oddly they seem to like the drumstick more than the thigh (I have a theory that this is because the legs are portrayed as drumsticks in cartoons). Can be puréed or chopped and frozen for babies and toddlers.

Serves 2

Sides Nothing is needed. Romaine or baby gem for something crisp

Prep/cooking time 45–50 mins

Active time 15–20 mins

. . . .

300ml chicken stock or broth, fresh (p.16) or made with powder/cube/paste

200g small salad potatoes, each cut in half

1 medium red pepper, de-seeded, halved lengthways and cut into 1cm slices

1 medium red onion (about 150g), peeled and cut into 5mm slices

3 garlic cloves, peeled and finely sliced

⅛ tsp salt

★ 50g lemon butter (p.64)

2 chicken legs, 200g each

2 tbsp chopped chives

Salt and cayenne pepper

1. Preheat your oven to 220°C/Gas 7, rack position upper middle shelf.

2. Get a medium-sized (20cm) ovenproof frying or sauté pan. Add the chicken broth. Put it onto a high heat. Reduce by half. Take the pan off the heat.

3. Add the potatoes, cut-side down, to the reduced chicken broth. Spread the pepper, onion and garlic over the top.

4. Sprinkle them with ⅛ tsp salt and a pinch of cayenne pepper, more if you want it spicy.

5. Cut 30g of the lemon butter into dice. Scatter it over the top.

6. Cover the pan tightly with foil. Put the pan onto a high heat. Bring to the boil. You'll be able to hear this under the foil: if in doubt, it takes about 1½ minutes. Take the pan off the heat.

7. Rub each chicken leg with a pinch of salt, a pinch of cayenne and 10g lemon butter. Put the chicken legs, skin-side up, onto the foil. Put the pan into the oven to roast'n'braise for 20 minutes. Take the pan out of the oven. Put the chicken legs onto a plate. Cut a hole in the foil. Drain the chicken's cooking juices and fat through the hole into the pan. Throw the foil away. Put the chicken legs, skin-side up, onto the potato and pepper mixture. Roast'n'braise for 10 minutes.

8. Turn the oven off and leave the chicken to rest for 5 minutes. Take the pan out of the oven. Brush the chicken legs with their cooking juices and sprinkle over the chives. Serve straight from the pan.

Roast squash spelt 'risotto' with lemon butter & olives

Okay, it's not a risotto because there is no rice. I wrote that to draw you into the idea of a recipe based on spelt, which is my favourite grain. There is now an incredible range of grains to buy ready-cooked and often they are very good. But for less money (even if it takes you more time), you could cook a batch yourself and keep it in 250g portions in your Magic Freezer. You can also make this recipe with quinoa, freekeh, Puy lentils or wheatberries.

Serves 2

Sides A rocket salad to use up the rest of the pack

Prep/cooking time 25 mins

Active time 25 mins

. . . .

1 tbsp vegetable oil

½ small butternut squash, peeled, de-seeded and cut into 1cm dice (about 300-350g flesh)

2 garlic cloves, peeled and finely chopped

★ 75g lemon butter (p.64)

300ml vegetable stock or bouillon, fresh or made with powder/cube

1 x 250g pouch ready-to-eat spelt (or quinoa, freekeh, Puy lentils or wheatberries)

35g rocket (½ typical packet)

125g ricotta cheese

10 black olives, pitted and halved

Salt and cayenne pepper

1. Start with the squash. Get a medium to large (24-26cm) frying pan. Add the oil and get it really hot. Add the diced squash. Season with salt and cayenne pepper. Fry over a medium heat for 3 minutes, enough to brown it around the edges. Turn the heat to low. Add the chopped garlic and 25g of the lemon butter. Sauté for 30 seconds, being very careful that the butter and garlic don't burn.

2. Add the stock. Bring to the boil. Lower the heat to medium. Simmer for 5 minutes or until the squash is just tender.

3. Add the spelt and bring back to the boil. Simmer for 2 minutes. Stir in the rocket. Take the pan off the heat.

4. Stir in the rest of the lemon butter.

5. Season to taste with salt and cayenne pepper. Spoon the spelt onto plates. Spoon the ricotta in little dollops over the spelt. Scatter the olives over the top.

Cook extra

This reheats brilliantly. Make twice the recipe, up to the point of adding the rocket at step 3, then freeze half or have it for lunch the next day.

RED CURRY PASTE

This is not Thai curry paste but my curry paste; it doesn't need to be red hot, and it is a combination of Thai and Middle Eastern ideas. My curry paste has the fragrance of lime leaf and lemongrass from the Thai version, and the creaminess of the Levantine pepper purée, muhammara. If you like it spicy, you can make a red-hot paste, or you can keep the heat gentle and the red curry paste can become a dip, or a sauce to toss with noodles like you would pesto.

Galangal doesn't give me the bite I like for this, I prefer ginger. Sometimes, when you buy lemongrass in supermarkets, it will come in a packet with a thumb-sized piece of galangal. Use that and top it up with ginger. If you are vegetarian, leave out the anchovies and replace the fish sauce with light soy.

Makes Approx. 500g (36 tbsp)

Storage Unopened, fridge 1 month. Opened, fridge 2-3 days. Freezer 3 months

Prep/cooking time 40 mins

Active time 30 mins

. . . .

2 large red peppers

1 tbsp vegetable oil, plus extra to cover the paste in jars

3 lemongrass stalks (30g), trimmed and sliced

3 kaffir lime leaves (dried are fine)

2-6 red chillies, depending on how hot you like it

5 garlic cloves, peeled

5 tsp peeled and chopped fresh root ginger

½ tsp ground cumin

1 tsp ground coriander

4 anchovies or ½ tsp shrimp paste

4 heaped tbsp soft brown sugar

3 tbsp Thai fish sauce

40g sundried tomatoes

2 tbsp tomato purée

Salt

1. Preheat your oven to 200°C/Gas 6, rack position upper middle shelf.

2. Start with the peppers. Cut them in half. Take out their seeds. Get an oven tray just large enough to hold them. Put the peppers on the tray. Brush the peppers all over, inside and out, with 1 tbsp vegetable oil. Season with salt. Roast skin-side down for 10 minutes. Turn the peppers. Roast for 10 minutes more.

3. While the peppers roast, put the other ingredients in your liquidiser.

4. Once the peppers are roasted, add them to the liquidiser. Blend for 2 minutes until the paste is smooth.

How to store

Store in clean, preferably sterilised jars, of the size that you are mostly likely to use up in one go. Fill the jars up to 2cm from the top. Pour over a layer of oil to seal the top: this stops the air getting to the paste and is vital. Cover the jars tightly with clingfilm first, then with a lid. Store in the fridge. You can also put some of the curry paste into very clean plastic containers, seal them with an airtight lid and freeze.

Once the curry paste is open, it can keep for 2-3 days, or even longer, but be very careful to make sure the sides of the jar are clean and you keep a piece of clingfilm directly touching the surface. The most important thing is to keep the air away from the food. Use a clean spoon and don't put your fingers into the paste unless you are going to finish the whole jar.

RED CURRY PASTE
MAGIC IDEAS

Curries made this way are excellent recipes to have in your repertoire of 'quick' meals. My versions are by no means traditional and I've made a few helpful discoveries along the way.

Once you add the chicken, prawns or fish, be careful not to boil or even simmer them, this makes them tough and dry. Simply poach them through, very gently, and you will be rewarded with protein that is tender and juicy.

I often hear and read about the importance of frying curry paste before you make the curry. I prefer not to do this. I think it's more important to add a little curry paste at the end of the cooking time to refresh each recipe before serving. This brings the original flavour to the fore and gives you a delightfully fresh curry.

RED CHICKEN CURRY

Serve this curry with rice. This curry, and all variations opposite, serve 2.

Prep/cooking time 25-30 mins
Active time 20-25 mins

. . . .

2 x 150-175g skinless chicken breasts, cut into 2.5cm dice

★ 9 tsp red curry paste (p.76)

¼ tsp salt

200ml coconut milk

100ml vegetable or chicken stock or broth, fresh (p.16) or made with powder/cube/paste

160g green vegetables (broccoli, peas, beans)

Salt

1. Start with the chicken. Put it into a bowl. Add 2 tsp curry paste and ¼ tsp salt. Mix until the chicken is well coated with the paste. Boil your kettle.

2. Get a small saucepan. Add the coconut cream, stock and 4 tsp paste. Bring to the boil. Lower the heat to medium. Simmer for 1 minute. Add the chicken. Cover, but leave the lid slightly ajar. Poach (the liquid must not boil) over a low heat for 8 minutes or until the chicken is just cooked through. Turn off the heat. Cover. Leave to rest for 2-3 minutes.

3. Get a large pot. Fill it with boiling water from your kettle. Add salt. Bring to the boil. Add the vegetables and boil for 3-5 minutes or until tender. Drain. Put them back into the pan. Sauté for 20-30 seconds to evaporate the last of the water and intensify the vegetables' flavour. Turn off the heat. Add 1 tsp curry paste. Toss until the vegetables are coated with the paste. Season with salt.

4. Stir 2 tsp curry paste into the chicken. Season with salt. Put the vegetables on top. Serve from the pan.

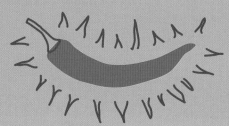

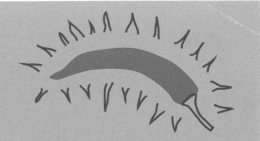

PRAWN CURRY Simmer the coconut milk, stock and paste for 4 minutes. Replace the chicken with 10 small or 5 large prawns per person. Poach for 2-3 minutes depending on the prawns' size. Just make sure they change colour from clear to pink. Rest for 2 minutes. Continue as the chicken recipe opposite.

SALMON CURRY The same method and cooking time as the prawn curry, using 300g salmon cut into 5cm pieces in place of the prawns.

VEGETABLE AND TOFU CURRY Simmer the coconut milk, stock and paste for 4 minutes. Replace the chicken with 200g tofu cut into 2cm dice (mix this very gently with the curry paste). Add to the coconut milk and poach for 2 minutes. Raise the quantity of green vegetables to 200g.

SWEET POTATO, PEPPER AND LENTIL CURRY Halve and de-seed a red pepper. Peel 350g sweet potatoes. Chop both into 3cm chunks. Toss with 1 tbsp vegetable oil. Roast at 200°C/Gas 6 for 20-25 minutes until golden and soft. Simmer the coconut milk, stock and paste for 4 minutes. Stir in 250g cooked lentils. Simmer for 1 minute. Toss the sweet potatoes and peppers with curry paste. Put them on top. Sprinkle with sliced spring onion.

Crab & red curry giant couscousotto

One of the great risottos is made with crustacean stock. The rice takes on an apricot colour as it cooks and becomes so highly perfumed with the lobster, crab or prawn that you don't actually need the crustacean's flesh. The only problem is that sometimes it takes on a stewed taste by the time the rice is cooked. To combat this, I use giant couscous, which cooks more quickly than traditional risotto rice, so I can keep the fresh shellfish flavour. The combination of brown crab meat and curry paste makes the couscous taste as if it has shellfish stock in it.

This is no good to purée for babies but great to serve as it is for toddlers. Wholewheat giant couscous is a wonderful base with which to introduce any sort of protein or vegetable to kids.

Serves 2

Sides Nothing is needed

Prep/cooking time 20 mins

Active time 20 mins

....

500ml vegetable stock or bouillon, fresh or made with powder/cube

2 tbsp extra virgin olive oil

2 garlic cloves, peeled and finely sliced

200g white or wholewheat giant couscous

150g frozen peas

Brown and white meat from 1 dressed crab (150-200g)

★ 5 tbsp red curry paste (p.76)

Salt and cayenne pepper or piment d'Espelette

1. Boil your kettle. Put a colander in your sink.

2. Start with the giant couscous. Get a small (16-18cm) saucepan. Add the stock, extra virgin olive oil and garlic. Put the pan onto a high heat. Bring to the boil. Add the giant couscous.

3. Bring back to the boil. Boil furiously for 1 minute. Turn the heat down to low. Put a lid on and simmer gently for 5 minutes (7 if the giant couscous is wholewheat). Top up with boiling water from your kettle if the couscous starts to dry out. Take the lid off. Stir and simmer for 3 minutes. Put the lid back and leave to sit for 2 minutes.

4. Fill a small (16-18cm) pan with water from your kettle. Add salt. Bring to the boil. Boil the peas for 3 minutes. Drain the peas in your colander.

5. Once the giant couscous is cooked, stir in the crab meat, red curry paste and the boiled peas. Warm the couscousotto through. If you'd like the consistency a bit more liquid, add hot water 1 tbsp at a time. Season to taste with salt and cayenne pepper or piment d'Espelette.

Cook extra

Cook twice the recipe and freeze half. The peas will discolour slightly when you reheat the giant couscousotto, but it'll still taste lovely.

Gurnard, red curry & mussel boil'n'braise

This is inspired by bouillabaisse. I boil the mussels, then braise the fish to provide the stock that flavours the soup that both are served in, and everything enhances everything else. The chickpeas provide the ballast and the red curry gives it a kick. The simplicity is astonishing and the variations are endless. I have a soft spot for gurnard: it's a charismatic fish, winged and wonderful, with a wise face and a wonderful head for fish soup. Gurnard flesh is firm, moist and marvellous to braise, but the boil'n'braise would be good with mackerel, coley, pollock, sea bream or sea bass, or you could double the mussels.

Get kids eating mussels, it's fun and they (both the kids and the mussels) are the future of sustainable food.

Serves 2
Sides Nothing is needed
Prep/cooking time
　15–20 mins
Active time 15–20 mins

. . . .

500g mussels

200ml coconut milk

★ 4 tbsp red curry paste (p.76)

½ x 400g tin chickpeas with
　their liquid

200g gurnard, cut into
　10 even-sized pieces

2–3 coriander sprigs

Zest of ½ lemon and
　2 tbsp juice

Salt and cayenne pepper

1. Start with the mussels. Pull the hairy beards out of each mussel by pulling each one from the thin to the thick end of each shell. Put each mussel into your colander and throw away each beard as you go. Wash the mussels well, and enjoy the sound they make. If any are open, tap them lightly; if they don't close by themselves then throw them away. I usually lose 2–3 mussels per kilo like this.

2. Get a medium-sized (20cm) shallow pan that you have a lid for. Add the coconut milk. Whisk in the red curry paste. Bring to the boil over a high heat. Add the chickpeas and their liquid. Bring back to the boil.

3. Add the mussels. Bring back to the boil. Boil for 1–2 minutes or until the mussels open enough for you to see the flesh inside; it really does happen this quickly.

4. Push the mussels to the edges of the pan. Season the gurnard with salt and cayenne pepper. Put the gurnard on top of the cooking liquor in a single layer. Put the lid on and watch over the pan. Bring to the boil, then take the pan off the heat the second it does. Leave to poach for 3 minutes. Check, the gurnard will be just cooked through. Throw away any mussels that haven't opened.

5. Pick the leaves from the coriander sprigs and scatter over the dish. Use a zester or microplane to grate the lemon zest over the top. Sprinkle the lemon juice over everything.

Stilton & red curry parcels with two tomatoes

This is the most delicious, if surprising, crunchy cheese special. If blue cheese is not your thing, replace it with goat's cheese, Camembert, or a mixture of leftovers from a cheese board. It sounds odd to start with but when you think of the chutneys and piccalilli that are so often served with cheese then it's just a little imaginative step further to mix cheese and curry paste. The dressing is a wonderful Magic Fridge standby in its own right, great with anything from grilled fish to green salad, and a particular stunner with roast peppers and mozzarella.

I've found that kids love filo parcels but don't like strong-tasting surprises, so go easy with the blue cheese for them.

Serves 2 as a main course

Sides Nothing is needed

Prep/cooking time
20-25 mins

Active time 20-25 mins

. . . .

120g Stilton cheese

2 sheets filo pastry

1 small egg, beaten

★ 6 tsp red curry paste (p.76)

3 tbsp water

25g butter

120g tiny frozen peas
(petits pois)

Salt and freshly ground
black pepper

For the salad

1 very ripe beef tomato, thinly
sliced

★ 2 tbsp red curry paste (p.76)

1 tbsp red wine vinegar

3 tbsp extra virgin olive oil

10g sundried tomatoes, finely
chopped

30g Stilton cheese

2 tbsp sliced mint

1. Preheat your oven to 200°C/Gas 6, rack position upper middle shelf. Line a baking sheet with a re-usable non-stick mat.

2. Start with the parcels. Cut the 120g Stilton into 6 triangular pieces.

3. Set up your chopping board going lengthways away from you. Unroll the filo pastry. Peel off one sheet. Lay it on your board. Brush it with beaten egg. Cut the filo into 3 strips lengthways. Put a piece of Stilton on the bottom of each, leaving a 2cm border. If the Stilton is too big, squash it flat. Put 1 tsp curry paste on top.

4. Take the right corner of the filo. Fold it diagonally to your left, to enclose the filling and make a triangle. Press down to seal the edges. Turn the filo back over the opposite way. Fold again along the upper crease of the triangle. Keep folding in this way until you reach the end of the filo strip. Brush the outer surface with more egg. Put the parcels onto the lined baking sheet as you go. Repeat this until you have 6 parcels.

5. Bake for 10 minutes until golden. Don't worry if a little cheese spills out the sides, this sets hard like in the photo and is delicious.

6. To make the mushy peas, get a small (16-18cm) pan. Add the 3 tbsp water and the butter. Bring to the boil. Add the peas. Bring back to the boil and boil rapidly for 1 minute. Mash the peas to a chunky texture. Season to taste.

7. Spread the sliced tomatoes around the insides of your plates. Get a small bowl, and add the red curry paste, vinegar, extra virgin olive oil and sundried tomatoes. Season to taste. Brush this all over the tomatoes. Break the 30g Stilton into tiny chunks over the tomatoes. Sprinkle the mint over the top.

8. Scatter the mushy peas over everything. Put the Stilton parcels on top.

Marinated tofu 'steak' with sesame & mango salsa

This idea came from an eating holiday with my best mate, Justin North, in Tokyo. We went to a tofu restaurant where the climax of many courses was a giant and glorious piece of tofu braised in soya milk. I like the idea of a vegetarian dish that is a big chunk of something you have to cut. The size is also an advantage when you cook the tofu because rather than having to turn or toss lots of little bits, you only have one large piece per person to deal with.

Tofu is great for kids, but give it to younger ones in small pieces or they'll struggle with the texture.

Serves 2

Sides Red, black or brown rice

Prep/cooking time 30 mins (plus marinating)

Active time 30 mins

. . . .

1 x 350–400g piece tofu

4 tbsp lime juice (1½ limes)

6 tbsp red curry paste (p.76)

40g sesame seeds

½ medium red onion (about 75g), peeled and thinly sliced

½ tsp caster sugar

100g mango flesh (about ½ small one), cut into 1cm dice

2 tbsp extra virgin olive oil

1 baby gem lettuce, large leaves separated (you need 6), hearts sliced

2 tbsp vegetable oil

60g beansprouts

50g peanuts (pre-salted are fine)

2 tbsp sliced mint

Salt, cayenne pepper and powdered seaweed (optional)

1. Start with the tofu. Cut it in half through the middle. Dry it as well as you can with kitchen paper. Put the two halves on a plate. Brush each tofu steak all over with 1 tbsp lime juice. Season with salt, cayenne pepper and powdered seaweed (optional) to taste. Brush each piece all over with 1½ tbsp curry paste. Scatter half of the sesame seeds over the tofu. Press the seeds in gently. Turn both pieces of tofu over. Scatter and press the second half of the seeds on the second side. Leave to marinate for at least 10 minutes and up to a day.

2. While the tofu marinates, make the mango salsa. Get a medium-sized bowl. Add the sliced onion, a pinch of salt, ½ tsp sugar, 1 tbsp curry paste and 2 tbsp lime juice. Leave to sit for 5 minutes to soften the onions. Add the mango and the extra virgin olive oil. Season to taste.

3. Put the baby gem onto one side of your plates.

4. Get a non-stick pan just large enough to hold the tofu comfortably. Add the vegetable oil and get it really hot. Carefully put the tofu steaks into the pan, you need to hear a very strong sizzle. Turn the heat down to medium. Fry for 3–4 minutes on each side until the sesame seeds are golden – turn the heat to low if you need to. Put the tofu next to the baby gem on your plates.

5. Add the beansprouts and peanuts to the pan. Sauté for 1 minute over a high heat, just to warm them through. Take the pan off the heat. Add the mint.

6. Scatter the beansprouts, peanuts and mint over the baby gem. Spoon the salsa over the top. Serve each tofu steak with 1 tbsp red curry paste on the side.

SOY & HONEY GLAZE

Soy, ginger, citrus and honey must have been the start of my love affair with the irresistible contrast of sweet and sour. The gloss of the glaze gets your juices flowing, then the taste follows its promise through. The glaze will transform a plateful of noodles, lentils or rice. A touch of the magic mixture will season hot or cold broccoli, cabbage, pak-choi, Chinese cabbage or choi-sum. It can be a baked- or roasted-on glaze for gammon, duck or pork. You can use it wherever you would soy sauce, and the reward for your work is the extra vigour of the honey, garlic and ginger.

Kids love this mixture, but just use small amounts for them. Preferably use low-salt soy sauce, as the reduced glaze becomes quite salty and the less salty their food the better.

Makes 400ml

Storage Fridge 2 months
at least. Freezer 6 months

Prep/cooking time
15–20 mins

Active time 15–20 mins

....

200ml balsamic vinegar (or spiced black rice vinegar)

200ml dark soy sauce

200ml orange juice (from a carton is fine)

200g honey (measure directly into your pan to avoid a sticky mess)

1 heaped tbsp peeled and grated fresh root ginger

4 garlic cloves, peeled and finely chopped

1. Get a medium-sized (20cm) straight-sided saucepan with a heavy bottom. Add the vinegar, soy sauce, orange juice, honey, ginger and garlic.

2. Bring to the boil over a high heat. Boil until the mixture has reduced by half and is thick enough to lightly coat the back of a spoon. Take the pan off the heat.

How to store

Pour the glaze when it is still warm because it thickens as it cools, which makes filling the bottles more difficult. Pour into sterilised jars or bottles and leave it to cool completely. Cover with very clean lids. Refrigerate. You can also put some of the soy glaze into very clean plastic containers, seal them with an airtight lid and freeze.

SOY & HONEY GLAZE
MAGIC IDEAS

Soy, honey and ginger are strong tastes, flavour 'changers' rather than delicate seasonings, which means the glaze will be the first and last thing you taste, no matter what you combine it with. The glaze is excellent with oily fish like mackerel, salmon, sardines and herring, crunchy vegetables like pak-choi, Chinese cabbage and choi-sum, and rich meats like duck and pork. It will liven up noodles and rice as you would expect, but more surprisingly, it'll also enhance lentils, especially black beluga lentils.

SOY & HONEY DIP The glaze makes a lovely dip because it has a texture that clings to things. Prawn crackers are a personal favourite. Carrots, radishes, baby gem quarters, mouli, peppers and pak-choi leaves are also very good.

SOY & HONEY STIR-FRIES Add a few spoonfuls to your wok just before serving your stir-fry. This seasons your ingredients and means you don't need to add the ginger and garlic at the start that so often end up burnt. The glaze can also be used to marinate thin slices of pork, chicken, beef or cubes of tofu to add to your stir-fry.

SOY & HONEY SALAD DRESSINGS For a traditional taste, try ⅓ sesame oil, ⅓ vegetable oil and ⅓ soy and honey glaze; season with chilli, lime and coriander. For a more fusion-inspired version mix ⅔ extra virgin olive oil with ⅓ soy and honey glaze then season with chilli, basil and lemon.

SOY & HONEY BARBECUE (OR GRILLPAN) MARINADE OR GLAZE This is an ideal marinade for barbecued chicken, pork, beef, burgers, sausages, prawns, squid or aubergines. You can marinate the ingredients in the glaze for up to a few days before grilling, or you can brush it over them as you grill for a more lightly charred taste. It's also lovely to have a bowlful of the glaze on the side to brush food with as it cooks.

AUBERGINE 'STEAK' WITH A SOY & HONEY GLAZE This is a lovely way of serving a large piece of vegetable just as you would a piece of meat. The soy and honey glaze lends a juicy, meat-like exterior. Cut an aubergine in half. Put the halves cut-side up on a lined baking tray. Criss-cross the flesh with a sharp knife. Brush generously with soy and honey glaze. Bake at 220°C/Gas 7 for 20–25 minutes until the aubergine flesh is soft and creamy. Brush the aubergine a second time with the glaze before you serve it.

BROCCOLI OR CAULIFLOWER 'STEAK' WITH A SOY & HONEY GLAZE

Braise a half broccoli or cauliflower head in foaming butter over a low heat with a lid on for 15-20 minutes until the cut face of the broccoli or cauliflower is golden brown and the whole thing is tender. Be careful of the temperature as it can burn quickly. Brush the florets with the soy and honey glaze as they braise. Brush the cut side once you turn it onto the plate. Sprinkle with citrus salt (p.258), if you like.

SWEDE 'STEAK' WITH A SOY & HONEY GLAZE

Peel the swede. Cut 2 thick slices out of the centre. Grate the remainder to serve as a coleslaw on the side. Simmer the 2 central slices until the swede is tender. Drain and dry the swede. Put it into a frying pan with soy and honey glaze and a touch of sesame oil. Fry the swede over a gentle heat, constantly basting it. Once glazed, dip the slices into sesame seeds then serve with the swede coleslaw.

MUSHROOM 'STEAK' WITH A SOY & HONEY GLAZE

Brush giant mushrooms all over with soy and honey glaze. Bake them hollow-side up with more soy and honey glaze in the hollow. You can put cooked rice or grains in the hollow or the mushroom 'steaks' can be used as the buns for bread-free burgers.

Liver with soy & honey glaze, bacon & apple

This is a new way to look at everyday liver. Fancy liver, foie gras, almost invariably has sweet accompaniments, and the onions often served with liver can be sweet, so why not a honey glaze? Apple and bacon are the cosy companions that I've added to ease you into the idea of liver with soy. As a general rule, the paler the liver, the more delicate the flavour. I look at liver as a treat, it's inexpensive, tasty and very good for you.

For something to become familiar, kids need to try it again and again, to eat it slowly with the other ingredients on their plate. I learnt that it is worth cutting it into small pieces to give them enough, but not too much, to chew on at one time. Take out the bacon, then this is good to purée or chop and freeze for toddlers.

Serves 2

Sides Nothing is needed

Prep/cooking time 20–25 mins

Active time 20–25 mins

. . . .

1 tsp vegetable oil, plus 1 tbsp

60g bacon lardons

100g peeled, cored and diced apple

100g spinach, washed and dried

125g (½ pouch) ready-to-eat lentils

250g pork or lamb's liver, cut into 1.5cm thick slices

★ 3 tbsp soy and honey glaze (p.88)

2 tbsp sesame seeds

Salt and Chinese 5-spice powder

1. Preheat your oven to 60°C/Gas as low as possible, rack position middle shelf.

2. Get a frying pan just large enough to hold the liver. Add 1 tsp vegetable oil and get it really hot. Add the bacon and diced apple. Sauté for 2 minutes until they start to brown around the edges. Add the spinach and cooked lentils. Sauté for 1½ minutes or just long enough to wilt the spinach and warm the lentils. Transfer to serving plates. Keep the mixture warm in your preheated oven. (Once you get confident with this recipe, you can do the spinach mixture in one pan while frying the liver in another, but it's better to start with one pan, at a gentler pace, so as not to overcook the liver and overheat yourself.)

3. Wipe out the frying pan, add 1 tbsp vegetable oil and get it really hot, as hot as you can. Put a plate with a rack on it next to your cooker.

4. Season the liver lightly with salt and Chinese 5-spice. Fry the liver for 1½ minutes over a medium to high heat. Turn the liver. Fry for 1 minute. Put the liver on the rack over the plate, and pour the fat over the top of it.

5. Add the soy and honey glaze and the sesame seeds to the pan. Bring to the boil.

6. Put the liver into the glaze. Take the pan off the heat. Turn the liver in the glaze until it is well coated, then quickly put it on top of the spinach and lentil mix.

7. Spoon the glaze that remains in the pan over the top.

Sardines with soy & honey glaze, grapefruit & wasabi yoghurt

I can't get enough of sardines: grilled, glazed, barbecued, baked, fried, fritters, hot, cold, warm or even tinned. I'm happy to eat them whole, but I know this doesn't appeal to everyone, so if you can get a fishmonger to 'butterfly' them, you not only have big boneless sardines, but a pretty presentation. There will always be tiny bones; eat these up, they're almost imperceptible and incredibly good for you.

Mangetout make speedy finger food and lovely language fun with kids as they translate to 'eat everything'. The sardines, but not the salad, are good to purée or chop and freeze for babies and toddlers. Just be aware that amongst the little bones there may be a few big ones.

Serves 2

Sides Nothing is needed.
   Plain grains or egg noodles
   for bulk

Prep/cooking time
   25–30 mins

Active time 25–30 mins

. . . .

100g beansprouts

100g pak-choi, leaves
   separated and cut into
   about 5cm pieces, the
   smaller leaves whole

50g mangetout

6 radishes, thinly sliced

1 tbsp sesame seeds

2 tbsp sliced mint

1 red grapefruit

4 tbsp plain yoghurt

½ tsp wasabi paste

6–8 sardines, butterflied,
   approx. 120g per portion

★ 3 tbsp soy and honey glaze
   (p.88)

1. Preheat your grill to its hottest setting, rack position upper middle shelf.

2. Start with the salad. Put the beansprouts, pak-choi, mangetout, radishes, sesame seeds and mint into a shallow dish.

3. Peel the grapefruit. Separate the segments as if you were going to eat them like an orange. Put half of the segments in your fridge for breakfast tomorrow. Slice the second half of the segments into 5mm slices widthways. Add them to the salad. Set aside.

4. Mix the yoghurt with the wasabi.

5. Pat the sardine fillets on both sides with kitchen paper to get them as dry as possible. Put them, flesh-side up, onto a baking sheet with a lip. Brush the sardine fillets with 1 tbsp soy and honey glaze on the flesh side. Turn the sardines so that they are skin-side up. Brush the skin with 1 tbsp soy and honey glaze.

6. Grill the sardines for 3–4 minutes – yes, it is this quick – until they are cooked through and nicely glazed on top. Please keep a close eye on the sardines – grills vary enormously so you might need to grill yours lower, higher, longer or more quickly. Feel free to mark the exact time and height for yours on this page. Take the sardines out from under the grill.

7. Toss the salad with 1 tbsp soy and honey glaze. Put the sardines on top along with any cooking juices from the baking tray.

8. Serve with the wasabi yoghurt on the side.

Cook extra

Flake the sardines then try this combination cold in a wrap or noodle salad. Keep the glaze on the side to mix with the salad or dip the wrap in.

Sticky soy, honey & ginger chicken with noodles

These chicken legs get gloriously sticky on the outside and suck the sweet and sour glaze into their flesh as they bake. The glaze provides the topping, sauce and a dressing for the noodles, the lemon a fresh and balancing burst to finish.

Eating noodles can be a great game for kids. It's worth trying to get kids to eat chicken on the bone, but I never insist as it adds tension to mealtimes. So if it becomes tricky, chop up the chicken and mix it with the noodles, you will still get them used to eating different tastes and textures. This dish (minus the bones) is good to purée or chop and freeze for babies and toddlers.

Serves 2

Sides Nothing is needed

Prep/cooking time
   35–45 mins

Active time 25–35 mins

. . . .

1 tbsp vegetable oil

2 chicken legs, 200g each

★ 3 tbsp soy and honey glaze
   (p.88)

1 large carrot (150g), peeled
   and sliced into thick ribbons
   with a vegetable peeler

1 small or ½ large red
   pepper, de-seeded and cut
   into 1cm slices

Zest of 1 lemon and juice
   of ½ (1½ tbsp)

2 nests medium egg noodles

120g tenderstem broccoli
   (or normal broccoli florets
   and stalk)

2 tsp sesame oil

Salt

1. Preheat your oven to 200°C/Gas 6, rack position upper middle shelf. Boil your kettle. Put a colander in your sink.

2. Start with the chicken legs. Put a small bowl to drain the fat into and a plate next to your cooker. Get a medium-sized (20cm) ovenproof frying pan. Add then heat the oil. Season the chicken legs with salt. Add them to the pan, skin-side down. Fry over a medium to high heat for 5–7 minutes until the skin is golden. Turn the chicken legs. Fry for 1 minute on the flesh side. Put the chicken legs onto the plate. Drain the fat into the small bowl.

3. Add the soy and honey glaze to the pan. Take the pan off the heat. Put the carrot and the sliced pepper into the pan in a single layer. Add the chicken legs to the pan, skin-side down. Put the pan in the oven for 10 minutes.

4. After 10 minutes, turn the chicken legs so that they are skin-side up on top of the pepper and carrot. Zest or grate half of the lemon zest onto the chicken skin. Bake for 10 minutes more. Turn the oven off, and leave the door slightly ajar.

5. After the chicken has been in the oven for 5 minutes, fill a large pot with water from your kettle. Bring it to the boil. Add salt, and bring back to the boil. Add the noodles. Cover the pot. Bring back to the boil. Boil for 1 minute. Add the broccoli. Bring back to the boil. Boil for 2 minutes. Drain.

6. Get the pan out of the oven. Transfer the chicken legs to a plate. Add the noodles, broccoli and sesame oil to the pan, and toss well. Put the chicken legs back on top. Grate or zest the rest of the lemon zest, and then squeeze the juice over the top.

Cook extra

The chicken legs are very nice cold. Cut off the meat to use in a wrap, noodle, rice or grain salad. You can double the recipe as it freezes and reheats very well.

Soy & honey-glazed beetroot with carrot & quinoa coleslaw

There is a trendy preparation called beetroot steak, which is a beetroot, roasted and squashed hard to firm its flesh and concentrate its flavour. I love this playful idea, but it involves a lot of trimming which is a complicated mess at home, so I've done a simplified version. The beetroot is my meat, quinoa the spuds and coleslaw the veg. The soy and honey give the beetroot a glossy glaze and a splash of gravy. Keep cooked beetroot in vacuum packs in your Magic Fridge and use this recipe as a starting point for adventures. When whole beetroot are in season, I like to cook them with their stalks on.

Beetroot is brilliant for kids, full of goodies, sweet and versatile. For younger kids, use less of the glaze. Leave the raw carrots out and this is good to purée or chop and freeze for babies and toddlers.

Serves 2

Sides Nothing is needed

Prep/cooking time
25–30 mins

Active time 25 mins

. . . .

450g cooked beetroot, peeled

4 tbsp soy and honey glaze (p.88)

Zest of 1 large lime and 3 tbsp juice

100g sour cream

1 large carrot (150g), peeled

125g (½ pouch) ready-to-eat quinoa (or lentils, or mixed grains)

Salt and freshly ground black pepper

1. Preheat your oven to 200°C/Gas 6, rack position upper middle shelf.

2. Start with the beetroot. Separate them into 300g and 150g. (If they are different sizes, I cut the smaller ones in half and grate the larger one.) Cut the 300g in half. Put the halved beetroot, cut-side down, into an ovenproof pan or tray just large enough to hold them. Add 2 tbsp soy and honey glaze. Brush the beetroot all over until they are well coated in the glaze. Roast in your preheated oven for 12–15 minutes until the glaze has reduced and the cut faces of the beetroot are shiny.

3. While the beetroot roast, get a medium-sized shallow bowl and a small bowl. Grate the zest of ½ the lime into each bowl, then squeeze the lime. Add 1 tbsp juice to the small bowl. Add 2 tbsp juice (or whatever remains if there is more) to the medium-sized bowl. Stir the sour cream into the small bowl. Season to taste with salt. Put the sour cream in the fridge until you need it.

4. Next, make the coleslaw. Grate (or use a mandolin to make little strips) the 150g beetroot and the carrot into the medium-sized bowl. Add the quinoa. Stir together well. Season to taste.

5. Put the coleslaw onto plates. Put the roast beetroot on top. Spoon the remaining 2 tbsp glaze over everything. Serve with the lime sour cream.

Cook extra

This is great cold, so make enough to have a portion for lunch the next day.

BAKED BEANS

Baked beans are a convenience food for most of us. When we don't feel like cooking we open a tin and have beans on toast. Both beans in tins and convenience foods are often considered bad, but I can happily rave about both: it's all about context, content and regularity. Now that I have my own baked beans (that aren't really baked) in my Magic Freezer, I am astounded at the range of tricks they offer me. Make sure they give you a meal before you freeze them: either make one of the recipes or have a great bowlful with a fried egg and cheese on top.

This recipe is particularly exciting for kids to be involved in: they can see how the beans swell when they soak overnight, then grow again and change colour as they cook. Baked beans are also a great way to introduce new vegetables to kids and good to purée or chop and freeze for babies and toddlers.

Makes 2.5kg

Storage Fridge 2-3 days. Freezer 3 months

Prep/cooking time 1¹/₂-1³/₄ hours, plus 12 hours for soaking the beans

Active time 30 mins

500g dried haricot beans

2 bay leaves

4 tbsp extra virgin olive oil

3 medium-sized onions (450-525g), peeled and finely chopped

8 garlic cloves, peeled and finely sliced

4 tbsp water

2 x 400g tins chopped tomatoes in juice

Salt, caster sugar and cayenne pepper or piment d'Espelette

1. Soak the beans for 12 hours in a large (24cm) pot of cold water.

2. Drain the beans in a colander. Rinse them thoroughly. Put them back into the pot. Barely cover the beans with fresh cold water, just enough to submerge them: too much water and they will become too liquid and tasteless; too little and the beans won't cook properly. Bring to the boil over a high heat. Add the bay leaves. Put a lid on the pan, but leave it slightly ajar. Turn the heat down to medium. Simmer very gently for 35-45 minutes (this will vary depending on the age of the beans) or until the beans are almost tender.

3. While the beans simmer, get a large (24cm) saucepan. Add the extra virgin olive oil, onions, garlic and water. Put the lid on and sweat for 6-8 minutes until the vegetables are soft. Add the tinned tomatoes and bring to the boil. Simmer for 5 minutes. Take the pan off the heat.

4. When the beans have simmered for 35-45 minutes and are almost tender, add the tomato sauce mixture. Simmer for 15 minutes more, or until the beans are tender.

5. Take the pan off the heat. Season with salt, sugar and cayenne pepper. Put the lid on. Leave to sit for 25 minutes.

How to store

I upcycle plastic takeaway containers with tight-fitting lids to store my beans in. A great upside to these is that they are microwavable. Spoon the beans with even amounts of their cooking juice in 300g portions (the following recipes all use 300g) into your very clean plastic containers. Leave to cool completely, do not touch the beans with your fingers. Cover the containers tightly. Refrigerate and/or freeze.

BAKED BEANS
MAGIC IDEAS

To discover a range of new ideas for baked beans, I had to go well beyond the bacon and sausage comfort zone. As it turns out, the beans are extremely adaptable, brilliant with seafood, and particularly good with my boil'n'braise technique below. You can adjust the beans' flavour by adding a great range of seasonings and the best way to do this is to add the different ingredients in quantities to your taste. Try chopped herbs like basil, parsley, thyme, rosemary and chives. Freshen the beans up with grated lemon zest, orange zest, fresh chilli or chopped tomatoes. Make them taste like smoky chorizo with smoked paprika, give them a scent of the south of France with herbes de Provence, or a taste of India with curry powder.

MUSSEL AND BEAN BOIL'N'BRAISE Put the beans into a shallow pan. Add enough tomato juice to make them slightly saucy. Bring to the boil. Add mussels, cover the pan and boil rapidly for 3-4 minutes until the mussels open. Throw away any that don't. Take the pan off the heat. Leave for 2 minutes to let the flavours soak into the beans. Sprinkle chopped chives over the top.

PRAWN, BACON AND BEAN BOIL'N'BRAISE Heat a large frying pan and sauté bacon lardons until golden. Add prawns. Fry one side of the prawns only, seasoning with cayenne pepper or chilli. Add the baked beans and a touch of water. Bring to the boil. Take the pan off the heat. Leave for 2 minutes to let the flavours soak into the beans. Season again to taste. Sprinkle sliced flat-leaf parsley over the top.

KEDGEREE BOIL'N'BRAISE Add enough milk to the beans to make them saucy. Add turmeric and curry powder to taste. Bring to the boil. Add some frozen peas. Bring back to the boil. Press bite-sized chunks of smoked haddock into the beans. Put the lid on. Turn the heat right down to braise the haddock for 5-6 minutes. I like to serve this with poached, rather than the traditional boiled, eggs on top. Sprinkle chopped chives over the eggs.

NEW ORLEANS CRAB BOIL'N'BRAISE The crustaceans in New Orleans are often boiled with a spice mix called 'crab boil', made of mustard seeds, coriander seeds, allspice, cloves, dried chilli pepper, bay leaves and cayenne pepper. You can buy this spice mix online or make your own, to season the beans. Heat the beans, then add the spice mix to taste with enough tomato juice to make it saucy. Stir in brown and white crab meat and serve mayonnaise on the side.

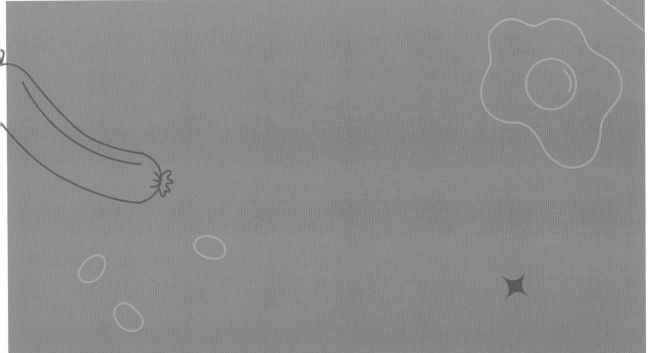

LEFTOVER MEAT AND BEANS
Leftover chicken, lamb, beef, sausages, pork and bacon can be stirred into the beans. These are my favourite ways:

Spanish beans: Add tinned chopped tomatoes and their juice to the beans. Bring to the boil then add the leftover meat in bite-sized pieces. Season to taste with any of the cayenne/Espelette/chilli/paprika family. Bring back to the boil. Put a lid on the pan and leave to sit for 2–3 minutes to finish heating through.

Tagine beans: Add chicken stock, ras-el-hanout, raisins and chopped dried apricots to the beans. Bring to the boil. Add bite-sized pieces of leftover roast lamb, chicken or turkey. Bring back to the boil. Add some chopped black olives and mint for a little taste of a tagine.

MOVE AROUND YOUR MAGIC FRIDGE
Season your beans with basil pistou (p.28), tomato chilli relish (p.124) or lemon butter (p.64).

Provençal beans: Stir ratatouille (p.112), halved black olives and extra virgin olive oil into the beans. Sprinkle with sliced basil or Provençal breadcrumbs (p.148).

Red curry beans: Stir a little red curry paste (p.76) into the beans along with a bunch of spring onions, thickly sliced. Sprinkle with sliced coriander.

Curried bean & chicken roast'n'braise with mushrooms

A chicken curry with a difference, this recipe continues my roast'n'braise exploration. It's a brilliant way to cook chicken legs, and the beans do some seriously good stuff with the porcini underneath. You can replace the curry powder with smoked paprika for a Basque version, or dried herbes de Provence for a robust taste of southern France.

I like kids picking up chicken legs and gnawing the meat off the bone, the more they chew the better! Great to purée or chop and freeze for babies and toddlers.

Serves 2

Sides Nothing is needed

Prep/cooking time
45–50 mins

Active time 15–20 mins

. . . .

 300g baked beans with their liquid (p.100)

100ml chicken stock or broth, fresh (p.16) or made with powder/cube/paste

10g dried porcini mushrooms

100g button mushrooms, washed

½ tsp curry powder

2 chicken legs, 200g each

2 tsp vegetable oil

40ml double cream

4 tbsp sliced flat-leaf parsley

Salt and curry powder

1. Preheat your oven to 220°C/Gas 7, rack position upper middle shelf.

2. Get a medium-sized (20cm) ovenproof frying or sauté pan. Add the baked beans, chicken stock, porcini, button mushrooms and curry powder.

3. Cover the pan tightly with foil. Put the pan onto a high heat. Bring to the boil, you'll be able to hear this under the foil; if in doubt, it takes about 1½ minutes. Take the pan off the heat.

4. Rub each chicken leg with 1 tsp oil, a pinch of salt and a pinch of curry powder. Put the chicken legs, skin-side up, onto the foil and put the pan in the oven. Roast'n'braise for 20 minutes. Take the pan out of the oven. Put the chicken legs onto a plate. Cut a hole in the foil. Drain the chicken's cooking juices and fat through the hole into the pan. Throw the foil away. Put the chicken legs, skin-side up, onto the beans. Roast'n'braise for 10 minutes.

5. Turn the oven off and leave the chicken to rest for 5 minutes. Take the pan out of the oven. Brush the chicken legs with their cooking juices. Spoon the double cream over everything. Bring to the boil. Scatter the parsley over the top. Serve straight from the pan.

Cook extra

Make as much as you can up to the point of adding the cream and parsley. Chicken legs freeze very well.

Full English cassoulet

From British breakfast to New Orleans brunch to dinner in Toulouse, pork and beans is as popular as a combination can be. Add an egg and I am not sure that there is anything better to eat. In this recipe the yolk mingles with the beans to make a creamy sauce. This is such a satisfying plate of food and one that's almost infinitely variable: you can add garlic sausage, chorizo, slices of belly pork, peppers, courgettes or cabbage. It's a dish to be eaten with a hearty appetite, when you have nothing to do afterwards but be contented.

Go easy on the amount of sausages, bacon and any cured meat you give younger kids; it's salty stuff, so small amounts with lots of beans and tomatoes is better. Good to purée or chop and freeze for babies and toddlers.

Serves 2
Sides Nothing is needed
Prep/cooking time 20 mins
Active time 15-20 mins

. . . .

2 tsp vegetable oil, plus 1 tbsp

6 smoked streaky bacon rashers, cut in half

6 chipolata sausages

80g button mushrooms

100ml chicken stock or broth, fresh (p.16) or made with powder/cube/paste

★ 300g baked beans with their liquid (p.100)

80g baby plum tomatoes

1 tsp dried herbes de Provence or thyme

2 large eggs

4 tbsp chopped chives

2 tbsp dried breadcrumbs

Salt and freshly ground black pepper

1. Get a medium-sized (20cm) frying pan. Add the 2 tsp vegetable oil and get it really hot. Add the bacon and fry on one side for 1 minute. Take the bacon out of the pan and put it on a plate.

2. Add the chipolatas to the pan. Fry for 2 minutes, turning the chipolatas once. Add the mushrooms and fry for 1 minute more. Add the chicken stock. Bring to the boil. Add the beans and bring to the boil. Add the baby plum tomatoes, herbes de Provence and bacon. Bring back to the boil. Turn the heat down to low. Simmer for 6 minutes. Season to taste.

3. After 3-4 minutes, get a non-stick frying pan just large enough to hold the eggs. Add the 1 tbsp vegetable oil and warm it. Break the eggs into the frying pan. Turn the heat down to low. Fry the eggs for 1½ -2 minutes until the white is just set and the yolk is still very runny.

4. Spoon the cassoulet into hot plates. Put the eggs on one side. Scatter the chives and breadcrumbs over the top.

Cook extra

Make as much as you can up to the point of adding the eggs and freeze as ready meals.

Braised halibut with summer bean 'stew'

This halibut is beautifully fresh and delicate. Braising beats poaching and steaming as my favourite light method of cooking fish; no flavour is lost, the juices mingle and the fish is exquisite. This play on a cassoulet is vibrant and variable: you could include broad beans and peas in spring, and pea shoots would be lovely to scatter over the top.

The halibut, bean and tomato mixture is good to purée or chop and freeze for babies and toddlers.

Serves 2
Sides Nothing is needed
Prep/cooking time 25 mins
Active time 20 mins

. . . .

★ 300g baked beans with their liquid (p.100)

100ml vegetable stock or bouillon, fresh or made with powder/cube

100g piquillo or other jarred peppers, drained and thickly sliced

125g baby plum tomatoes, cut in half

2 x 125g halibut, pollock or cod fillets

1 tbsp extra virgin olive oil

100g young runner beans, thinly sliced

4 tbsp sliced basil

Salt and freshly ground black pepper

1. Preheat your oven to 200°C/Gas 6, rack position upper middle shelf. Boil your kettle.

2. Get a large (24-30cm) shallow ovenproof frying or sauté pan. Add the baked beans and the vegetable stock. Bring to the boil. Add the peppers and baby plum tomatoes.

3. Brush the halibut fillets with the extra virgin olive oil. Season the fillets on both sides. Put them on top of the vegetables. Braise in your preheated oven for 6 minutes. Turn off the oven and leave the door slightly ajar. Leave the halibut to rest for 4 minutes, or until you are ready with the runner beans.

4. While the halibut braises, fill a large (24cm) pan with boiling water from your kettle. Add salt. Put a lid on and bring to the boil. Put a colander in your sink. Boil the runner beans for 4-5 minutes until they are tender. Drain in the colander.

5. Once the halibut is braised, transfer to deep plates with a fish slice. Gently fold the runner beans and basil into the tomato and bean mixture. Season to taste. Spoon the sauce all over and around the halibut.

Baked kippers with bean 'champ', garlic & lemon butter

Kippers are herrings that are split, cured and smoked. They are excellent at any time (not just for breakfast), and particularly when they are slathered with garlic and butter. The bean champ is a fast and feisty accompaniment, and the lemon butter is glorious with garlic and beans.

With kids, I suggest putting the kippers on a separate plate then taking the bones out together at the table. I like to make it into a game. Without the bones this makes an excellent meal to purée or chop for babies and toddlers. Both kippers and champ can be frozen.

Serves 2

Sides Nothing is needed

Prep/cooking time
15-20 mins

Active time 15-20 mins

. . . .

2 kippers

80g soft butter

3 garlic cloves, peeled and
finely chopped

6 spring onions (½ bunch),
trimmed

4 tbsp water

★ 300g baked beans with their
liquid (p.100)

4 tbsp milk

Zest and juice of ½ lemon

Salt and freshly ground
black pepper

1. Preheat your oven to 160°C/Gas 3, rack position upper middle shelf.

2. Start with the kippers. Get a baking tray just large enough to hold them. Put the kippers on top. Spread a quarter of the butter and garlic over each kipper. Bake for 10 minutes.

3. While the kippers bake, prepare the champ. Slice the spring onions thinly. Keep the dark green slices on one side of your chopping board to add to the butter at the end. Put the white and pale green slices and the rest of the garlic into a medium-sized (20cm) saucepan. Add 4 tbsp water.

4. Put the lid on the pan. Put the pan onto a medium heat. Sweat for 4 minutes until soft. Stir twice. If the onions start to dry out, add 2 tbsp more water. Add the beans and milk to the pan. Raise the heat and bring to the boil. Boil for 1 minute until the milk has reduced by half. Take the pan off the heat.

5. Crush the beans with a potato masher, just enough to break them open: don't mix too much or the beans will become gluey. Season to taste.

6. When the kippers have baked for 10 minutes, spoon the bean 'champ' into their cavity.

7. Put the rest of the butter and garlic plus the green spring onion into the empty pan. Zest or grate the lemon zest into the pan. Squeeze in the juice. Melt together and season to taste. Spoon the lemon butter over the kippers. Serve.

RATATOUILLE

Ratatouille encapsulates my philosophy of 'sunshine food' in a brightly coloured carnival of tomatoes, aubergines, courgettes and peppers. A gathering of vegetables so scented, evocative and enjoyable to cook that it was the original reason I fell in love with Provence.

Ratatouille is wonderful for kids, easy to eat, soft enough to be gentle on tiny teeth but still with just enough bite to get them working. You introduce kids to garlic and five vegetables in one hit.

Makes Approx. 1.6 kg

Storage Fridge 3 days. Freezer 3 months

Prep/cooking time 50–60 mins

Active time 30–35 mins

· ·

3 medium onions (approx. 450–525g), peeled and cut into 2cm chunks

8 garlic cloves, peeled and sliced

3 red and/or yellow peppers, halved, de-seeded and cut into 2cm chunks

4 tbsp olive oil

100ml water

1 tbsp tomato purée

3 strips dried orange peel or 6 fresh

1 tsp salt

½ tsp caster sugar

1 large firm aubergine (approx. 420g)

2 medium-sized firm courgettes

1 x 400g tin chopped tomatoes in juice

4 tbsp vegetable oil

Salt, caster sugar and cayenne pepper

1. Get a large (24cm) saucepan. Add the onions, garlic, peppers, olive oil, water, tomato purée and orange peel. Add 1 tsp salt, ½ tsp sugar and a pinch of cayenne pepper. Put the pan onto a medium heat. Put the lid on. Sweat for 12 minutes, stirring occasionally.

2. While the onion mixture sweats, prepare the aubergines and courgettes. Cut the green top off the aubergine. Cut it in half so that each half sits flat on your board. Then cut the aubergine lengthways into 2cm wide slices, then widthways into 2cm chunks. Cut the courgettes in half lengthways. Cut each half into 2cm slices on an angle.

3. Add the tinned tomatoes with their juice to the sweated onion mixture. Bring slowly to the boil.

4. Meanwhile, heat a large (30cm) frying pan with 3 tbsp of the vegetable oil. Add the aubergine chunks in a single layer. Fry for 4–5 minutes until they are gently browned. Season with salt. Add the fried aubergine to the onion mixture once it has sweated for 12 minutes and you've added the tomatoes. Cover with greaseproof paper and simmer over a medium heat for 20 minutes. Lift the paper and stir from time to time to make sure the ratatouille doesn't stick to the bottom of the pan.

5. Wipe out the frying pan. Add 1 tbsp vegetable oil. Add the courgettes and fry over a medium heat for 3–4 minutes until they are tender but not starting to brown. Season with salt. Transfer the courgettes to a plate.

6. Once it has simmered for 20 minutes, take the paper off the aubergine mixture. Add the courgettes. Stir them in. Simmer for 5 minutes more. Pick out and throw away the orange peel.

7. Taste, and season if necessary with salt, sugar to balance the tomatoes' acidity, and cayenne pepper for a little bite.

How to store

I upcycle plastic takeaway containers with tight-fitting lids to store my ratatouille in. A great upside to these is that they are microwavable. Spoon the ratatouille with even amounts of the cooking juice in 400g portions (the following recipes all use 400g) into your very clean plastic containers. Leave to cool completely, do not touch the mixture with your fingers. Cover the containers tightly. Refrigerate and/or freeze.

RATATOUILLE
MAGIC IDEAS

Once you've cooked your joyful pot of ratatouille, the possibilities are endless. Ratatouille can be made in great quantities and frozen. It can be served hot or cold, on its own or to liven up anything from fish to cheese to chicken. I love it for breakfast with eggs, I love it for lunch in a baguette that starts off crisp then softens as it irresistibly imbibes the rich ratatouille, and I love it for dinner with duck. Over the many years that I've made ratatouille, whatever I cook, scatter, serve alongside or on top, the flavour of the ratatouille sings happily through.

RATATOUILLE TART OR PIZZA
Top a circle or square of puff pastry or pizza dough with an even layer of ratatouille. Crumble soft goat's cheese over the ratatouille. Bake the tart for 18-20 minutes at 190°C/Gas 5 or until the pastry is crisp and the cheese golden. Scatter sliced basil or spoon basil pistou (p.28) over the top.

RATATOUILLE SANDWICH
Open a baguette without cutting it all the way through, and douse the inside with extra virgin olive oil. Go on, a bit more! Press the bread inside the crust to make a hollow. Brush it with a cut garlic clove. Stuff it with ratatouille and scatter sliced basil or spoon pistou (p.28) over the top. Close it up then press hard to get the juices soaking into the bread. The longer you leave it, the more deeply the ratatouille soaks in. Take the biggest bite you can.

RATATOUILLE GRATIN
Spread ratatouille into a baking dish. Mix in chopped black olives. Top with diced mozzarella. Bake the gratin for 15 minutes at 190°C/Gas 5, or microwave on high for 2-3 minutes then grill for 2-3 minutes. The mozzarella will be golden topped and oozing into the ratatouille. Eat the gratin with a salad or some hot bread and extra virgin olive oil.

RATATOUILLE AND FISH EN PAPILLOTE
Spoon ratatouille over half of a large piece of foil. Put a fillet of sea bream or sea bass on top. Brush extra virgin olive oil all over it. Fold the foil over the fish, then seal the foil package tightly. Bake at 200°C/Gas 6 for 12 minutes.

RATATOUILLE, PULSE OR GRAIN SALADS
Ratatouille is excellent as a seasoning for any sort of grain, from quinoa to white rice, and for pulses from borlotti beans to lentils or chickpeas. Warm your grain or pulse before you mix in the ratatouille so that it becomes more receptive and soaks up the seasonings.

RATATOUILLE WITH FETA
Warm a portion of ratatouille, sprinkle feta cubes and fresh basil over the top. Finish with a trickle of extra virgin olive oil.

RATATOUILLE AND CHEESE ON TOAST
You can go about this in a few different ways. Rub a halved baguette with garlic, spread with warmed ratatouille then bake with sliced Brie on top until the cheese melts into the ratatouille. Or grill the baguette with grated Cheddar on top of the ratatouille. Or you can spread the ratatouille onto a pitta bread or wrap, put well-dried chopped mozzarella on top, then bake it like a pizza.

RATATOUILLE WITH BURRATA
Ratatouille, extra virgin olive oil, burrata, fresh basil. Bliss.

SPEEDY RATATOUILLE FRITTATA
Preheat your grill and warm a 16–18cm non-stick pan with 1 tbsp extra virgin olive oil. Fry 200g ratatouille for a minute. Add 3 large eggs beaten with 2 tbsp sliced basil, salt and pepper. Fold the eggs over a high heat for 2 minutes until the mixture has almost set. Sprinkle with 2 tbsp freshly grated Parmesan. Grill for 2–3 minutes until lightly browned. Leave to sit off the heat for 5 minutes. Serve hot, warm or cold with extra virgin olive oil trickled over the top.

RATATOUILLE AND BEAN BAKE
Mix ratatouille with the baked beans (p.100) to serve as a hearty stew. Or spread the mixture into an ovenproof dish and top with grated cheese (or Provençal breadcrumbs, p.148). Bake at 190°C/Gas 5 for 20–25 minutes until golden.

RATATOUILLE AND PIZZA PIE
Use ratatouille to replace the stuffing for pizza pie (p.170).

SWEET AND SOUR RATATOUILLE
To transform ratatouille into a sweet and sour salad to serve cold with mozzarella or burrata, add sweet and sour pepper chutney (p.136) to taste.

LEMON RATATOUILLE
Stir lemon butter (p.64) into hot ratatouille. I use 12g butter per 100g ratatouille.

Chicken leg roast'n'braise with ratatouille & bacon

The ratatouille softens and stews in this recipe. The butter beans laze away underneath and soak it all up until they burst with flavour then take on the taste of the chicken and bacon at the end. I've cooked this recipe with chickpeas, haricot beans or cannellini beans in place of the butter beans and all are equally good. If you don't have an ovenproof frying pan, I'd strongly recommend getting one: it makes this type of recipe quicker, there is no temperature change to deal with, and there is less washing up at the end!

Leave out or eat all of the bacon then this dish can be chopped or puréed and frozen for babies and toddlers. Put their portions to one side before you season yours with salt and cayenne pepper.

Serves 2

Sides Nothing is needed

Prep/cooking time 35 mins

Active time 15-20 mins

. . . .

★ 400g ratatouille (p.112)

1 x 400g tin butter beans
  with their liquid

4 dry-cured streaky
  bacon rashers

2 large chicken legs,
  200g each

4-6 tsp extra virgin olive oil

Salt and cayenne pepper

1. Preheat your oven to 220°C/Gas 7, rack position upper middle shelf.

2. Get a medium-sized (20cm) ovenproof frying or sauté pan. Add the ratatouille and the butter beans with their liquid.

3. Cover the pan tightly with foil. Put the pan on a high heat. Bring to the boil, you'll be able to hear this under the foil; if in doubt, it takes about 1½ minutes. Take the pan off the heat. Put the bacon over the top of the foil.

4. Rub each chicken leg with 1 tsp extra virgin olive oil, a pinch of salt and a pinch of cayenne pepper. Put the chicken legs, skin-side up, onto the bacon on the foil. Roast'n'braise for 20 minutes. Take the pan out of the oven. Put the chicken legs onto a plate. Cut a hole in the foil. Drain the chicken's cooking juices and fat through the hole into the pan. Throw the foil away. Put the chicken legs, skin-side up, and the bacon onto the beans. Roast'n'braise for 10 minutes.

5. Turn the oven off and leave the chicken to rest for 5 minutes. Take the pan out of the oven. Trickle 1-2 tsp extra virgin olive oil (I like a lot) over each leg. Serve straight from the pan.

Cook extra

I always make more than I need of this. It freezes brilliantly and doesn't dry out. More magic to have on hand when you don't feel like cooking.

Braised mackerel with ratatouille, olives & walnuts

Braising fish gives you a great exchange of flavour between the fish and the ingredients it is braised on and in. The ratatouille becomes both braising liquor and vegetable accompaniment. I've cooked gurnard, red mullet, sea bass, sardines and sea bream fillets using this recipe, but mackerel is a family favourite. The way the colours combine is so beautiful that it's worth cooking this recipe just to gaze at it.

This can be chopped or puréed and frozen for babies and toddlers. Put theirs to one side before you season yours.

Serves 2

Sides Mashed potatoes made with olive oil instead of butter. Spelt or any other plain grain. Bread. Polenta

Prep/cooking time 20-30 mins

Active time 20 mins

....

★ 400g ratatouille (p.112)

3 tbsp extra virgin olive oil

2 tbsp water

4 tbsp sliced basil

4 mackerel fillets, skin on, 120-150g per portion

10 black olives, pitted and cut in half

8 walnut halves

Grated zest of ½ lemon and 1 tbsp lemon juice

Salt, caster sugar and cayenne pepper

1. Preheat your oven to 190°C/Gas 5, rack position upper middle shelf.

2. Get an ovenproof dish large enough to hold the mackerel fillets. Spread the ratatouille over its base. Stir in 1 tbsp extra virgin olive oil and 2 tbsp water. Put this into the preheated oven for 10 minutes until the ratatouille is hot. (If you've just made the ratatouille and it's already hot, you don't have to do this bit.)

3. Take the dish out of the oven. Stir in half the basil.

4. Season the mackerel fillets with salt and cayenne pepper. Put the mackerel fillets on top of the ratatouille mixture. Brush a little of the ratatouille juice over the mackerel. Braise for 6-7 minutes until the mackerel is just cooked through. Turn off the oven. Leave the door slightly open. Let the mackerel rest for 3 minutes.

5. While the mackerel braises, make the dressing. Get a small bowl. Add 2 tbsp extra virgin olive oil, the olives, walnuts, lemon zest, lemon juice and the rest of the sliced basil. Season to taste with salt, cayenne pepper and sugar to balance the lemon.

6. Once the mackerel is braised and rested, take it out of the oven. Spoon the dressing over the top and serve straight from the braising dish.

Ratatouille with Parmesan & fried eggs

I first came across this combination at a restaurant called Scarborough Fare near a beach in New Zealand. At the time I was obsessed by what I thought was interesting and exciting about food – rare ingredients, funky and often misplaced partnerships – so serving an egg at a restaurant seemed far too ordinary. Only later, when I'd eaten and cooked much more, did I understand the magic to be found in everyday ingredients. The way the egg yolk runs into the ratatouille casts a spell on me every time I break it. I love the contrast in texture between the chewy and crisp Parmesan, the soft ratatouille and runny egg. If you do not have a very good non-stick pan, do not attempt to fry the Parmesan as I do in the recipe. It will stick. Sprinkle the Parmesan over the top instead, it'll still be delicious.

Serves 2

Sides Any sort of soaker, bread, plain grains, simmered potatoes, or a green salad that you can toss in and coat with the juices

Prep/cooking time 10–15 mins

Active time 10–15 mins

. . . .

★ 400g ratatouille (p.112)

100g chorizo, cut into 5mm slices (optional, merguez is also lovely)

1 tbsp extra virgin olive oil

90g Parmesan cheese, freshly grated

4 tbsp small basil leaves

2 medium, very fresh eggs

Salt flakes and smoked paprika

1. Get a medium-sized (20cm) frying pan or dish that goes in the microwave. Add the ratatouille and the chorizo (if you want it). Heat the ratatouille for 2–3 minutes in the microwave or frying pan. Be sure not to heat it too long so that it stays nice and saucy.

2. Get a non-stick frying pan large enough to hold the eggs with a little space around the outside. Add the extra virgin olive oil and warm it for 20 seconds. Sprinkle half the Parmesan cheese in an even layer on each side of the pan, being sure to leave a 3cm gap in the middle so that it's easier to get the eggs out once they're cooked. Sprinkle two-thirds of the basil leaves into the cheese. Fry over a medium heat for 1 minute or until the Parmesan has melted.

3. Break an egg onto each side of melted Parmesan in the frying pan. Turn the heat down to low. Fry the eggs for 1½ –2 minutes until the white is just set and the yolk is still very runny. The eggs cook into the cheese which is chewy underneath and crisp around the outsides. Take the pan off the heat. Leave the eggs to sit for 1 minute.

4. Spoon the ratatouille onto one side of your plates.

5. Use a large spatula to transfer the eggs and their cheesy crisps next to the ratatouille. Season the eggs with salt flakes and smoked paprika. Scatter the rest of the basil leaves over the ratatouille.

Ratatouille & ricotta cannelloni

The ricotta sets off the ratatouille beautifully to make this recipe an irresistible mixture of soft, savoury, sweet and creamy. You could also use this combination with a twist to make a version for coeliacs: bake long slices of aubergine instead of pasta which you roll around the ricotta to serve as the cannelloni wrapper.

The cannelloni aren't good to chop or purée, but a version of this without the pasta makes a lovely standby for babies and toddlers.

Serves 2

Sides Nothing is needed, but a crisp green salad is nice

Prep/cooking time 45 mins

Active time 15-20 mins

. . . .

250g ricotta cheese

75g Parmesan cheese, freshly grated

4 tbsp sliced basil

6 x no-pre-cook cannelloni tubes

★ 400g ratatouille (p.112)

150ml tomato juice

2 tbsp extra virgin olive oil

Salt and freshly ground black pepper

1. Preheat your oven to 190°C/Gas 5, rack position middle shelf.

2. Start with the ricotta mixture. Get a large bowl. Add the ricotta, two-thirds of the grated Parmesan and the sliced basil. Mix together. Season to taste with salt and freshly ground black pepper. I like a lot of black pepper in this.

3. Using a small spoon, press this mixture into the cannelloni tubes. To make it easier push in half from the opening at one end and half from the other end. (If you have one, use a piping bag to do this, it is so much quicker and easier.)

4. Get an ovenproof dish just large enough to hold everything. Spread the ratatouille over its base. Put the cannelloni on top. Pour over the tomato juice. Brush the juice all over the cannelloni to soak and glaze them. Next, brush the extra virgin olive oil over the cannelloni.

5. Cover the ovenproof dish tightly with foil. Bake in your preheated oven for 25 minutes. Take the foil off. Sprinkle the rest of the Parmesan evenly over the cannelloni. Bake for 5 minutes more. Serve straight from the dish.

TOMATO CHILLI RELISH

This is a wonderful example of how recipes do the rounds. I've adapted the relish from a Delia Smith recipe for chilli jam. Delia adapted it from a recipe that she was given by Galton Blackiston at Morston Hall. Many thanks to both of them. I've tried this with dried chillies of all sorts, with fresh chilli too, but the best way to control the heat is to add chilli powder or cayenne pepper at the end. For a smoky flavour, this is also excellent made with smoked paprika. You need to stir the relish frequently and watch carefully as it starts to dry out; it will bubble up and can quickly catch on the bottom of the pan.

There are plenty of fun things to serve this with and along the way kids can get used to the taste of garlic and ginger, two ingredients that can light up their culinary lives for life. As you add the chilli at the end it's easy to make a kid's batch which is milder, with another one as hot as you like it. My kids find a little heat in their mouths funny, but too much is terrifying.

Makes About 300g (20 tbsp)

Storage Unopened, fridge 1 month. Opened, fridge 2-3 days. Freezer 6 months

Prep/cooking time 40-60 mins

Active time 15-20 mins

. . . .

1kg tomatoes

4 tbsp soft brown sugar

5 tbsp white or red wine vinegar

2 tbsp Thai fish sauce (or soy sauce for vegetarians)

2 tbsp peeled and grated fresh root ginger

4 large garlic cloves, peeled and finely sliced

5 tbsp extra virgin olive oil, plus extra to cover the mixture in your jars

Salt, caster sugar and chilli powder, cayenne pepper or smoked paprika

1. Use a little serrated knife with a sharp tip to cut out the green stem bit on top of the tomatoes. Put half of the tomatoes into your food processor with the rest of the ingredients, except for the seasoning. Blend them to a smooth purée.

2. Pour the purée into a large (24cm) shallow pan; the higher the sides of your pan are, the longer the mixture will take to reduce. Purée the second half of the tomatoes. I do this in two batches because it is very liquid and can make a real mess. Add the purée to the pan.

3. Put the pan on a high heat. Bring the relish to the boil; it should bubble all over. Turn the heat down to medium. Simmer the relish for about 30 minutes, stirring at least once every 5 minutes or it will catch on the bottom of the pan. (It can take longer and depends on how much water is in the tomatoes.) The tomato chilli relish is ready when a wooden spoon pulled through the middle of the pan leaves a line that caves in seconds after you make it.

4. Season and spice to taste with salt, sugar and chilli. Remember that the relish will get stronger and hotter as it ages.

How to store

Store in clean, preferably sterilised jars or bottles, of the size that you are most likely to use up in one go. Fill up to 2cm from the top. Pour over a layer of extra virgin olive oil to seal the top: this stops the air getting to the relish and is vital. Cover the jars or bottles tightly with clingfilm first, then with a lid. Store in the fridge. You can also put some of the relish into very clean plastic containers, seal them with an airtight lid and freeze.

Once the relish is open, it can keep for 2-3 days, or even longer, but be very careful to make sure the sides of the jar are clean and you keep a piece of clingfilm directly touching the surface. The most important thing is to keep the air away from the food. Use a clean spoon and don't put your fingers into the relish unless you are going to finish the whole jar.

TOMATO CHILLI RELISH
MAGIC IDEAS

The tomato chilli relish has sweet, sour and spicy notes, so it can add different things in different ways to different ingredients. The relish sets off less intensely flavoured ingredients like aubergine, squid or chicken, the sour and spicy notes contrast the richness of pork, duck and oily fish like mackerel, herring and sardines, or it can enhance the sweetness already present in crab or prawns. It can become a glaze, a marinade, a sauce or simply remain a relish. The combination of cheese and tomato has been my love for longest so I am going to concentrate on that partnership here.

GOAT'S CHEESE AND TOMATO CHILLI RELISH ON TOAST Spread tomato chilli relish on long croûtons made from a baguette (p.32). Top with slices of goat's cheese and bake the croûtons at 190°C/Gas 5 for 4–5 minutes until the cheese is hot. Serve with baby gem quarters dressed with olive oil and balsamic vinegar.

FIGS TOPPED WITH GOAT'S CHEESE AND TOMATO CHILLI RELISH Cut figs in half, spread them with tomato chilli relish and top with goat's cheese. Bake at 190°C/Gas 5 for 6–9 minutes, depending on how ripe the figs are, until they are soft, messy and runny. Trickle extra virgin olive oil over the top. Wrap a napkin around your neck and eat them as hot as you can.

CHEDDAR AND TOMATO CHILLI RELISH SANDWICH Tomato chilli relish goes wonderfully instead of pickle in a Cheddar cheese sandwich.

MOZZARELLA AND TOMATO CHILLI RELISH PITTA Spread tomato chilli relish over pitta bread, cover with fresh basil leaves, top with slices of mozzarella and bake at 220°C/Gas 7 for 12–14 minutes or until melted and moreish.

LETTUCE 'BREADLESS' OPEN SANDWICH Cut a romaine heart in half. Spread tomato chilli relish over it. Top with halved cherry tomatoes and grapes and cubes of feta. Trickle olive oil over. Sprinkle with salt flakes, or citrus salt (p.258).

CAMEMBERT BAKE WITH TOMATO CHILLI RELISH Slice a ripe Camembert in half horizontally and spread plenty of tomato chilli relish over the bottom half. Put the other half on top, make a few holes with a knife and pour over some olive oil and/or a little white wine. Wrap it all up in foil and bake at 180°C/Gas 4 for 20 minutes. Serve and eat quickly like a fondue with crispy bits of bread or hot simmered salad potatoes for dipping.

ROASTED PEPPERS WITH BLUE CHEESE AND TOMATO CHILLI RELISH
Halve, seed and then roast yellow peppers with olive oil, salt and sugar until soft. (Or used tinned or bottled peppers.) Fill the peppers with 2-3 tbsp tomato chilli relish, and crumble over enough soft blue cheese to cover the relish. Bake at 190°C/Gas 5 for 15-20 minutes or until everything heats up and oozes together wonderfully.

ROCKET, PARMESAN AND TOMATO CHILLI RELISH SALAD
Cut Parmesan flakes with a vegetable peeler. Toss with rocket, tomato chilli relish and a simple dressing of olive oil and balsamic vinegar.

CHEESY FLATBREAD WITH TOMATOES AND RELISH
Spread tomato chilli relish over a flatbread or wrap. Mix 2 parts mascarpone cheese with 1 part grated Parmesan. Add sliced basil, salt and freshly ground black pepper to taste. Spread this over the top of the flatbread or wrap, but leave a generous border. Scatter halved cherry tomatoes over the top and bake at 220°C/Gas 7 for 8-10 minutes.

MIXED CHEESE PIZZA WITH TOMATO AND CHILLI SAUCE
Spread a pizza base (p.160) with tomato chilli relish. Top with a mixture of blue, soft, cream, Cheddar and goat's cheeses. Sprinkle freshly grated Parmesan over the top before and after baking, at 200°C/Gas 6 for 15-20 minutes.

ROQUEFORT AND TOMATO CHILLI RELISH ON TOAST
Spread very good butter over very good raisin or fig toast. Spread a very thin layer of tomato chilli relish over the top. Put artistically cut slices of Roquefort on top. Sit there for a bit and eat slowly. If you have some sweet wine to go with it, then lucky you.

MUSSEL AND TOMATO CHILLI RELISH BOIL'N'BRAISE
Put a pile of cleaned mussels into a pan with just enough water to cover the base of the pan. Put on a tight-fitting lid, bring to the boil and boil over a high heat for 3-4 minutes until all the mussels are open (discard any that remain shut). Stir in some tomato chilli relish.

Crab, bean & tomato chilli relish cakes

Crab and fish cakes often have too much ballast, most commonly potato. It's a way of stretching the seafood and making the cakes easier to handle, but it also means that you end up with a dry, uninteresting plate of food. My cakes are a little harder to handle, but even if they end up a bit wobbly, you've got tons of taste and plenty of succulent filling. I have a real thing for hidden surprises, especially those that moisten and add flavour, so I've tucked some relish away in the middle.

Crab is a good food for kids; just be very careful to check for any traces of shell.

Serves 2
Sides Nothing is needed
Prep/cooking time 30 mins
Active time 25 mins

....

1 dressed crab (about 150g mixed white and brown meat)

1 x 400g tin haricot beans, thoroughly drained and patted dry with kitchen paper

¼ tsp smoked paprika

★ 7 tbsp tomato chilli relish (p.124)

Plain flour, for dusting

1 large egg

75g fresh breadcrumbs

2 tbsp vegetable oil

2 tbsp plain yoghurt

Grated zest of 1 lime and 2 tbsp juice, plus lime wedges to serve

40–50g watercress (½ typical packet)

Salt and smoked paprika

1. Preheat your oven to 200°C/Gas 6, rack position upper middle shelf.

2. Weigh the crab meat. Weigh the same quantity of drained and thoroughly patted dry haricot beans into a shallow dish. You will have some beans left over. Add the smoked paprika and 1 tbsp tomato chilli relish. Mash the beans with a fork until they are nearly puréed. Add the crab. Mix together well. Season to taste with salt.

3. Dust your hands with flour. Separate the mixture into 2 and shape into cakes of approximately 2.5cm thick. They are very soft at this stage, don't worry, they are meant to be.

4. Make a little hole in the middle of each cake and push 1 tbsp tomato chilli relish into each hole. With floured hands, push the crab mixture from the sides over the top so that the relish is covered and surrounded.

5. Beat the egg in a small bowl. Brush the beaten egg generously over the top and sides of each crab cake. Pat half of the breadcrumbs over the top, then, using a fish slice, turn each cake over and brush with egg wash. Coat the tops and sides with the rest of the breadcrumbs and press them on gently.

6. Get an ovenproof frying pan just large enough to hold the cakes. Add the vegetable oil and get it really hot. Fry the crab cakes for 1 minute. Turn the crab cakes with a strong, wide fish slice. Transfer the pan to the preheated oven and bake for 8 minutes.

7. Mix the yoghurt and 1 tbsp tomato chilli relish with the rest of the beans. Add the lime zest and juice. Season to taste.

8. Serve the bean salad with the crab cakes, watercress, lime wedges and the rest of the tomato relish.

Cheat's chorizo burger with tomato chilli relish & coleslaw

Combinations for new recipes can come from the most surprising places. The idea for this chorizo burger sprang from a vague memory of eating a square pork sausage on a night out in Glasgow, mixed with a recollection of a pintxos crawl in San Sebastian that starred a smoked paprika and apricot meatball in a brioche bun. I've served this patty in sesame buns, on fennel focaccia and wrapped in Chinese cabbage. All work very well.

The patty is good to purée or chop and freeze for babies and toddlers. It can then be mixed with vegetables, grains or pulses. Chinese cabbage or Chinese leaf makes a great finger food and holder: the crunchy stalk is juicy and the leaves make a good wrap. Use them in place of buns or wheat wraps from time to time.

Serves 2
Sides Nothing is needed
Prep/cooking time 30 mins
Active time 25–30 mins

. . . .

350g pork mince

Grated zest of ½ orange

★ 5 tbsp tomato chilli relish (p.124)

6 dried apricots, finely chopped

2 tsp smoked paprika

½ tsp salt

2 tsp vegetable oil

4 tbsp water

2 burger buns

1 medium carrot (100g), peeled

50g radishes

½ red pepper, de-seeded

1 tbsp extra virgin olive oil

Grated zest of ½ lemon and 2 tbsp juice

4 tbsp sliced mint

3 tbsp mayonnaise

Salt, caster sugar and smoked paprika

1. Put a rack on top of a plate next to your cooker to rest the burgers on.

2. Next, make the burgers. Get a shallow bowl. Add the mince, the orange zest, 2 tbsp of the tomato chilli relish, the chopped apricots, 2 tsp smoked paprika and ½ tsp salt. Mix enough to combine the ingredients but no longer or you'll make the burgers tough. Pat it into 2 x 2.5cm thick patties.

3. Get a frying pan just large enough to hold the burgers comfortably. Add then heat 2 tsp vegetable oil. Fry the burgers for 3 minutes each side, over a medium heat, for medium (63°C). Put the burgers on the rack over the plate to rest for 3–4 minutes.

4. Add 4 tbsp water to the pan, bring to the boil, and stir to get every last bit of meaty goodness from the pan. Brush the burgers with these pan juices to give them an intense glaze. Put the burger buns cut-sides down in the pan to warm them through slightly.

5. Start the coleslaw while the burgers cook. Slice the carrot into ribbons with a vegetable peeler. Cut the radishes into thin circles. Slice the pepper lengthways as thinly as you can. If you find it easier, you can grate the carrots and radishes, it's a little less crunchy, but equally nice. Put the prepared vegetables into a shallow bowl. Mix in 1 tbsp tomato chilli relish, the extra virgin olive oil, lemon zest, lemon juice and mint. Season to taste (use sugar to balance the lemon).

6. Mix the mayonnaise together with the rest of the tomato chilli relish. Spread the chilli relish mayonnaise across the buns. Make burgers with the patties. Serve the coleslaw on the side.

Mediterranean 'Bo Ssäm' – lettuce, chicken & tomato chilli relish wrap

I first came across the idea of using leaves as a wrap for meat on a Korean Airline flight and I love the tactile nature of it – like an easy way to roll sushi. The 'Bo Ssäm' can be made with any cooked or leftover meat: I've also made them with roast peppers, glazed aubergine or lentils as the main stuffing. Haloumi or mozzarella would be good too. The tomato chilli relish provides the punch in place of the traditional kimchi. I've extended this recipe to serve four, because it's ideal to share, and can be carried over to lunch the next day.

I've learnt that these 'build your own' dinners are great for kids. Many skills and pleasures that cooks need to develop are involved in making a wrap; smelling, tasting, touching, mixing, seasoning. Crisper lettuces like romaine, baby gem or Chinese cabbage are better for kids than soft lettuce because they enjoy the crunch, but find the leafy part hard to chew. Give them the lettuce to gnaw or suck on, then the rest can be good to purée or chop and freeze for babies and toddlers.

Serves 4

Sides Nothing is needed

Prep/cooking time 20-25 mins

Active time 20-25 mins

. . . .

★ 50g tomato chilli relish (p.124), plus 100g for serving

1 tbsp dark soy sauce

1 tbsp honey

2 small skinless chicken breasts, 150g each (or 300g of any cooked leftover meat)

1 large soft lettuce, leaves separated

1 x 250g pouch cooked lentils (or rice or quinoa)

100g radishes (1 average bunch or pack)

100g olives, pitted and halved

8 spring onions, finely sliced

Salt and cayenne pepper

1. Preheat your oven to 200°C/Gas 6, rack position upper middle shelf.

2. Get a small bowl. Mix the 50g tomato chilli relish with the soy sauce and honey.

3. Get a baking tray. Put the chicken breasts on it. Brush them all over with the relish, soy and honey mixture. Sprinkle salt and cayenne pepper evenly over both sides. Turn each breast shiny-side up, with the fatter end facing away from you on the baking tray. Put the tray in the preheated oven with this fatter end of the breasts towards the back.

4. Bake for 12 minutes. A cooked chicken breast feels firm to the touch. Turn the oven off. Open the door and leave it slightly ajar while the chicken rests for at least 5 minutes and as much as 10. It's also good cold.

5. While the chicken bakes, put bowls of the tomato chilli relish, lettuce, lentils (hot or cold, up to you), radishes, olives and spring onions on your table.

6. Once the chicken is cooked and rested, slice it thinly, and put it onto plates.

7. Wrap the chicken cheerfully at your table with tomato chilli relish for spice and sauce, lentils for ballast, olives for extra salt, radishes for more crunch and spring onions for a gentle bite.

Sautéed squid with tomato chilli relish, freekeh & fennel salad

Squid is an ingredient of extremes: it either needs to be fried in a flash or cooked slowly for a long time. The quick version suits the Magic Fridge best. The tomato relish gets transformed into a glaze for the squid and a spicy vinaigrette for the crisp salad. Cooked freekeh is available in pouches; it can be replaced with cooked spelt or quinoa in this salad.

I've learnt that the texture of squid takes some getting used to for kids, so start them off with tiny bits. This salad is no good to purée for babies but great to finely chop for toddlers. Chunks of fennel and pak-choi stalks make great finger food for teething kids to suck on, the fennel is sweet and the pak-choi very juicy and delicate.

Serves 2

Sides Nothing is needed, but if you're very hungry, double up the freekeh and add an extra tbsp of tomato relish

Prep/cooking time 20-25 mins

Active time 20-25 mins

. . . .

½ medium-sized fennel bulb

125g (½ pouch) ready-to-eat freekeh, wheatberries or spelt

2 tbsp lime juice, plus a little for seasoning the squid

2 tbsp extra virgin olive oil

2-3 heads baby pak-choi (about 100g), leaves separated

4 tbsp tomato chilli relish (p.124)

1 medium squid (approx. 250g) cleaned

1 tbsp vegetable oil

80g baby plum tomatoes, halved

80g chorizo, cut into 5mm slices

Salt, cayenne pepper and smoked paprika

1. Start with the salad. Put the half fennel bulb flat-side down on your chopping board. Slice it finely. Put the sliced fennel into a large shallow bowl. Add the freekeh, 2 tbsp lime juice and 2 tbsp extra virgin olive oil. Stir together well. Put the pak-choi, and 1 tbsp tomato chilli relish on top, but don't mix them for now so that the pak-choi stays crisp.

2. Use a sharp knife to open the squid tube so that it turns into a rough square. Score it in a criss-cross pattern on the inner side. Cut the squid tube into 3cm triangles and the tentacles into 5cm lengths.

3. Heat a large (30cm) frying pan with 1 tbsp vegetable oil until it begins to smoke. Add the squid in a single layer then leave for 30 seconds over your highest possible heat. Toss the squid then return to the heat for 30 seconds. Add 3 tbsp tomato chilli relish. Toss for 10 seconds, just long enough to glaze the squid. Take the pan off the heat. Season with salt, cayenne pepper and lime juice. Add the squid to the salad ingredients.

4. Add the tomatoes and chorizo to the pan. Toss over a high heat for 1 minute to warm them through.

5. Mix everything together in the shallow bowl. Season to taste with salt and smoked paprika. Serve.

SWEET & SOUR PEPPER CHUTNEY

Pepper chutney was an original standby in the Magic Fridge at my cookery school back in Provence. Its life began as an accompaniment to a red pepper soufflé, but since then I've used it with everything from slippery squid to creamy goat's cheese. The chutney appeals to my sweet and sour addiction, and it's so incredibly appetising and easy to make. The chutney can be made with any colour pepper except green; decades into my cooking career, the joyful mix of yellow and red still excites me.

Because the peppers are very soft in this chutney and the honey makes them sweet, it's a great way to introduce them to kids. Finely chopped, or puréed, the chutney beautifully seasons mash, polenta or grains for kids, as they start on food becoming ever more solid.

Makes 480-500g

Storage Unopened, fridge 2 weeks. Opened, fridge 2-3 days. Freezer 3 months

Prep/cooking time 35-40 mins

Active time 15-20 mins

. . . .

4 large orange, red or yellow peppers

4 garlic cloves, peeled

4 tbsp extra virgin olive oil

10 tbsp (150ml) water

8 tbsp (120ml) red wine vinegar

7 tbsp (105ml) clear honey

¼ tsp salt

Salt, caster sugar and cayenne pepper

1. Cut the peppers in half lengthways. Scoop out the seeds. Cut the halves in half again. Cut the pepper quarters into 5mm strips. Slice the garlic finely.

2. Get a medium-sized (20cm) shallow saucepan that you have a lid for. Put in the peppers, garlic, extra virgin olive oil, water, red wine vinegar, honey and ¼ tsp salt. Put the lid on.

3. Bring to the boil over a high heat. Turn the heat down to medium then simmer for 15 minutes or until the peppers are soft.

4. Once the peppers are soft, take the lid off. Turn the heat up to medium high. Boil until most of the liquid has evaporated (this takes 8-10 minutes) and the peppers are translucent and glazed with their cooking juices.

5. Take the pan off the heat. Season to taste with salt, sugar and cayenne pepper.

How to store

Store in clean, preferably sterilised jars, of the size that you are mostly likely to use up in one go (multiples of 120g are good for the following recipes). Fill the jars up to 2cm from the top. Cover the jars tightly with clingfilm first, then with a lid. Store in the fridge. You can also put some of the pepper chutney into very clean plastic containers, seal them with an airtight lid and freeze.

Once the pepper chutney is open, it can keep for 2-3 days, or even longer, but be very careful to make sure the sides of the jar are clean and you keep a piece of clingfilm directly touching the surface. The most important thing is to keep the air away from the food. Use a clean spoon and don't put your fingers into the chutney unless you are going to finish the whole jar.

SWEET & SOUR PEPPER CHUTNEY
MAGIC IDEAS

Sweet and sour pepper chutney enlivens foods that are delicate in flavour, but it's also bold enough to jostle for supremacy with stronger flavours. When you have ingredients that need a little something, that something is often pepper chutney. Fattier meats love sweet and sour, so you could even use it to replace your apple sauce for roast pork or duck.

SEAFOOD WITH SWEET & SOUR PEPPER CHUTNEY Any of the following seafood - fried or deep-fried - is lovely with a spoonful or two of pepper chutney on the side: prawns, squid, mackerel, herring, sardines, anchovies, salmon, crab (cold or in crab cakes), cooked mussel flesh.

GREEN SALAD WITH SWEET & SOUR PEPPER DRESSING Toss rocket and romaine or baby gem leaves with pepper chutney and balsamic vinegar. Add a herb from your windowsill: my favourites in green salad are chives and basil.

SWEET & SOUR GRAIN SALADS Toss pepper chutney with almost any cooked grain or small pasta. I've used quinoa, freekeh, couscous, giant couscous, spelt, Camargue red rice, black rice (this is very pretty with the peppers) and bulgur wheat. You can then add one of the following combinations: Grated carrot, beetroot or radish • Diced fennel, courgette or cucumber • Fresh, dried or sunblush tomato • Dried fruit • Spices like ras-el-hanout, sumac or smoked paprika. Add some fresh herbs for an excellent and original salad.

SWEET & SOUR SCRAMBLED EGGS AND OMELETTES Stir pepper chutney into eggs before you scramble them, or fold the chutney into the centre of an omelette.

SWEET & SOUR PEPPER FRITTATA Simmer 200g sliced salad potatoes for 15 minutes or until tender. Drain and mix them with 6 tbsp pepper chutney, 4 eggs, salt and cayenne pepper. Preheat your grill and warm a 20cm non-stick pan with 1 tbsp extra virgin olive oil. Add the egg mixture. Fold over a high heat for 2-3 minutes until the mixture has almost set. Sprinkle with 4 tbsp freshly grated Parmesan. Grill for 2-3 minutes until lightly browned. Leave to sit off the heat for 5 minutes. Serve hot, warm or cold with extra virgin olive oil.

CHEESES WITH SWEET & SOUR PEPPER CHUTNEY
Vibrant sweet and sour accompaniments are ideal to bring out the flavours and contrast the richness of cheese. Use halloumi, mozzarella or ricotta dressed with the chutney to make a light meal with some salad, or you can use the chutney as an accompaniment for a cheese board.

BRUSCHETTA WITH SWEET & SOUR PEPPER TOPPINGS
Get big slices of sourdough bread. Rub a halved garlic clove all over the bread. Brush oil over the top then grill the bread slices, preferably in a grill pan, griddle, panini maker or on a barbecue. Failing any of these, your oven grill will be fine. You build a salad of sorts on top of the grilled bread, and pepper chutney makes an ideal base and dressing for other ingredients:

Pepper chutney, bacon, lettuce, tomato and avocado

Pepper chutney, ricotta and basil (can add Parma or Bayonne ham)

Pepper chutney, smoked salmon and avocado

'Pulled' chicken and pepper chutney (shred roast chicken, stir in pepper chutney and balsamic)

Pepper chutney, grilled prawn, sundried tomato and baby plum tomato

ROMAINE LETTUCE 'BRUSCHETTA'
With so many people not eating bread these days, this is a great idea to have in your armoury. Here the crisp lettuce halves replace the bread. Cut the romaine heart in half lengthways, brush it with olive oil, then sit it on a plate, with the cut side facing up. Finely chop garlic and scatter it over the top. Sprinkle with salt flakes and piment d'Espelette or cayenne pepper. Top it with anything from the list above.

MOVE AROUND YOUR MAGIC FRIDGE
All the ideas here would work for the tomato chilli relish on p.124 as well.

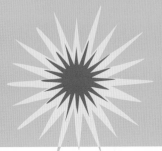

Crisp-skinned salmon with pepper chutney & olives

I learnt how to fry fish skin until it's properly crisp when I worked in Tours at 2-star-Michelin restaurant, Jean Bardet, and the Bistro Le Canotier that his daughter Valerie owned. The trick is to fry the fish over a medium rather than high heat to give the skin time to become crisp all the way through. If you fry it over too high a heat, the skin will go brown on top, but stay chewy underneath. Here, the sour part of the chutney becomes both glaze and sauce to cut through the fatty salmon wonderfully. I sometimes add a little diced chorizo to the peppers.

This is an excellent recipe to purée or chop and freeze for babies and toddlers.

Serves 2

Sides Red rice is particularly good, so is red or black quinoa, spelt, or a chunk of hot bread

Prep/cooking time 20 mins

Active time 20 mins

. . . .

2 tsp vegetable oil

2 x 150g salmon fillets, skin on

★ 120g sweet and sour pepper chutney (p.136)

100g baby plum tomatoes, cut in half

2 tbsp water

10 black olives, pitted and cut in half

1 tbsp extra virgin olive oil

4 tbsp sliced basil, plus a few small leaves to garnish

Salt and cayenne pepper

1. Get a non-stick frying pan just large enough to hold the salmon fillets. Spoon the oil into the pan and get it really hot.

2. Season the salmon fillets with salt and cayenne pepper. Put the salmon skin-side down into the pan. Turn the heat down to medium. Fry for 6 minutes over the medium heat until the skin is golden and crisp. You can go by sound and sight: there should be a healthy sizzle but you shouldn't see any smoke.

3. After the 6 minutes, brush the salmon's flesh side all over with the juice from the pepper chutney. Turn the salmon over. Raise the heat to high. Fry for 30 seconds. Put the salmon on plates.

4. Add the pepper chutney to the pan. Add the halved baby plum tomatoes, 2 tbsp water, black olives and the extra virgin olive oil. Bring to the boil. Boil for 30 seconds. Take the pan off the heat.

5. Add the sliced basil. Season the chutney/salsa to taste. Spoon it next to the salmon but not over the top so that you don't soften the crisp skin. Sprinkle a few little basil leaves over everything.

Cook extra

Leave a portion of salmon to go cold. This would make an excellent salad, either mixed with greens or grains. One fillet is enough for two grain salads.

Crunchy lettuce, prawn, chorizo & pepper chutney salad

I cut baby gem, chicory or romaine hearts into wedges rather than separate them into leaves to make a salad base with great structure and crunch. It looks lovely and lets you prepare the lettuce hours ahead. Pork and prawns have become a clichéd combination with good reason, they love each other; here the pork is chorizo and the pepper chutney brings the two even closer together.

I've learnt that giving younger kids crunchy, rather than soft, salad inspires them to eat more of it. Prawns are a challenge for kids because of their texture. I introduced them to my boys over a couple of years and they fight me for every prawn now.

Serves 2

Sides Grilled bread, fried potatoes or couscous

Prep/cooking time 15-20 mins

Active time 15-20 mins

....

20g sundried tomatoes, soaked in 100ml boiling water for 10 minutes

1 baby gem lettuce, cut into 6 wedges

1 red or white chicory (or a second baby gem), cut into 4 wedges

1 tbsp vegetable oil

10 large raw tiger prawns, heads and shells taken off (freeze those for a stock), black veins cut out

50g chorizo, thinly sliced

80g baby plum tomatoes, halved

★ 120g sweet and sour pepper chutney (p.136)

2 tbsp lemon juice

2 tbsp water

2 tbsp extra virgin olive oil

40g radishes, thinly sliced

Salt and cayenne pepper

1. Prepare all of the ingredients before you start to cook as it goes very quickly at high temperature once you begin. I like to line the ingredients up next to my cooker in the order I am going to add them to the pan.

2. Drain the sundried tomatoes. Slice them into thin strips. Put 3 wedges of baby gem and 2 of red chicory on each of your plates.

3. Get a large frying pan. Add the vegetable oil and get it really hot. Add the prawns. Fry for 30 seconds over a high heat. Add the sliced chorizo, and fry for 30 seconds more. Turn the prawns. Add the baby plum and sundried tomatoes and the pepper chutney. Toss over a high heat for 1 minute. Season with very little salt and cayenne pepper to spice it up.

4. Scatter the prawns, chorizo, tomatoes and pepper chutney over and around the baby gem and chicory wedges. Add the water, lemon juice and extra virgin olive oil to the pan. Put the pan back onto a medium heat. Scrape the bottom with a wooden spoon to get all the caramelised goodies. Spoon these juices over the salad.

5. Scatter the sliced radishes over the top. Serve.

Roast duck breast with figs, pepper chutney & watercress

The light bite of the pepper chutney makes it an exciting partner for duck. Once you've tried my way of cooking duck breasts they'll become a regular part of your repertoire. Delia Smith loved it so much at one of our food and wine workshops that she now uses my technique for her own recipes. The crisp skin is thin; the meat is lean, moist and in love with the sweet and sour peppers and spicy watercress. The duck leaves you with some golden fat to sauté a future feast of mushrooms, potatoes or eggs.

Serves 2

Sides Quinoa, spelt, beetroot, carrots

Prep/cooking time 30-40 mins

Active time 15-20 mins

....

2 duck breasts

2 figs, cut in quarters

★ 120g sweet and sour pepper chutney (p.136)

2 tbsp water

2 tbsp extra virgin olive oil

1 tbsp lemon juice

100g watercress, spinach or a mixture

4 tbsp pomegranate seeds (you can buy ready-seeded)

Salt, salt flakes and cayenne pepper

1. Preheat your oven to 200°C/Gas 6, rack position upper middle shelf. Put a small cooling rack over the top of a plate next to your cooker.

2. Get an ovenproof frying pan just large enough to hold the duck breasts. Put the duck breasts into the pan, skin-side down. Put the pan onto a medium heat and fry for 10 minutes until the skin is golden brown. Put the pan in the oven and roast for 6 minutes for duck that is perfectly pink. Take the pan out of the oven. Turn the oven off.

3. Next, using a pair of tongs, put the duck breasts, skin-side up, onto the cooling rack over the top of the plate. Put the plate and rack with the duck breasts back in the oven to rest for 8 minutes. Leave the oven door slightly open so that it is warm rather than hot.

4. Drain half of the fat from the pan into a heatproof container. Add the quartered figs to the pan. Sauté over a high heat for 1 minute. Add the pepper chutney, 2 tbsp water and the the extra virgin olive oil to the pan. Bring to the boil. Season to taste with lemon juice, salt and cayenne pepper. Take the pan off the heat.

5. Put the watercress onto your plates. Slice each duck breast into 7 slices. Season the sliced duck with salt flakes. Put the slices on top of the watercress. Spoon the pepper chutney and fig mixture over the top. Scatter the pomegranate seeds over everything.

Cook extra

You don't even need to cook extra; you could cut a few slices off each breast to save for lunch the next day. Cut the slices into small dice, then mix them with cooked grains, dried or fresh figs, grated beetroot or carrot, some of the chutney and a warm spice like ras-el-hanout.

Upside-down pepper chutney, ricotta & beetroot tart

An upside-down tart is generally like a tarte Tatin that is cooked upside down but then turned over. It can be quite hard to keep the pastry crisp until the last minute, so why not just add it at the last minute? Here the topping and fillings go on the plate, the pastry gets cooked separately and then put on top just before you serve it. The pastry goes upside down and stays there. It's a technique that opens up all sorts of possibilities.

I've learnt that adding pastry in any way helps introduce kids to new foods. In this case you could get them to put almost any sort of healthy seed on top of the pastry as a safe and fun way to get them involved. Let them crunch on the pastry separately then the rest is good to purée or chop and freeze for babies and toddlers.

Serves 2

Sides Nothing is needed. A bit of bread if you are really hungry

Prep/cooking time 25 mins

Active time 25 mins

....

1 sheet filo pastry

1 tbsp extra virgin olive oil, plus extra for brushing

1 tsp fennel seeds

★ 120g sweet and sour pepper chutney (p.136)

125g ricotta cheese

60g Parmesan cheese, freshly grated

4 tbsp sliced basil

200g cooked beetroot

1 baby gem lettuce, cut into 4 wedges

2 tsp balsamic syrup

Salt and freshly ground black pepper

1. Preheat your oven to 175°C/Gas 3½, rack position upper middle shelf. Put a cooling rack next to your cooker.

2. Start with the pastry. Get a baking sheet. Line it with a re-usable non-stick mat – this pastry is impossible to get off anything that is not non-stick.

3. Put the filo sheet onto your chopping board. Cut it in half. Brush one half with about 1 tsp extra virgin olive oil. Put the second half on top. Brush with extra virgin olive oil. Cut out 2 double-layer 10cm circles from the pastry. Put these onto your lined baking sheet. Sprinkle the fennel seeds over the top.

4. Weigh out 30g of pepper slices from the chutney. Spread them very evenly in a single layer over the top of the pastry circles.

5. Bake for 10 minutes in your preheated oven until the pastry is golden. Use a palette knife to transfer the pastry to a cooling rack while it is still warm so that it doesn't stick.

6. While the pastry is baking, make the cheese mixture. Get a small bowl. Add the ricotta, Parmesan and sliced basil. Mix together. Season to taste.

7. Slice the beetroot as thinly as you can. Spread the slices all over your plates. Season with salt and pepper. Put 2 baby gem quarters flat-side down, side by side, in the middle of each plate. Spread the ricotta mixture over the top.

8. Trickle a ½ tbsp extra virgin olive oil over each plate, followed by 1 tsp balsamic syrup.

9. When you are ready to serve, put the pastry on top of the ricotta mixture and press it gently so that it sticks. Serve the rest of the pepper chutney alongside.

PROVENÇAL BREADCRUMBS

I didn't learn to make these breadcrumbs in Provence, but with Raymond Blanc in Oxfordshire. His focus was freshness, the amount of parsley he used was more than I'd seen before, the scent was more evocative than I'd smelt before and the taste was more intoxicating than I thought possible. Keep your old bits of bread and freeze them until you have enough to dry them in a low oven and make these crumbs. The bread needs to be well dried so that its crunch can come through the parsley.

Kids love crunchy stuff, so these crumbs are a good way to introduce them to herbs. At a time when it seems to me that a lot of kids' food is breadcrumbed, why not make the crumbs magically turn green!

Makes 400g

Storage Freezer 3 months

Prep/cooking time
1 hour 15 mins

Active time 15 mins

. . . .

200g white bread (weight before drying)

150g parsley

20g dried thyme or savory leaves, or herbes de Provence

6 garlic cloves, peeled

4 tbsp extra virgin olive oil

Salt and freshly ground black pepper

1. Preheat your oven to 100°C/Gas the lowest possible, rack position middle shelf.

2. Cut the bread into small (3cm) dice. Put the bread onto a baking tray. Dry in the oven for 1 hour or until the bread is totally dry. Take the dry bread out of the oven and leave it to cool.

3. Set up your food processor. Put the parsley, thyme and garlic into the bowl. Blend for a minute or so until everything is finely chopped. Crush the dried bread a little with your hands. Add it to the herb mixture. Use the pulse button to blend everything to a coarse texture and bright green colour. I prefer the breadcrumbs not to be too finely chopped so that they keep more crunch.

4. Add the extra virgin olive oil. Pulse to combine. Season to taste.

How to store

Store your Provençal breadcrumbs in airtight containers in the freezer. They will stay green, be free-flow and easy to get out of the containers. There is no advantage to storing them in the fridge.

PROVENÇAL BREADCRUMBS
MAGIC IDEAS

Provençal breadcrumbs are much more than just a crunchy coating. Adventure beyond their traditional uses and there's a lot of fun to be had. You can scatter them into salads, over the top of stews and soups, on gratins, on cheese on toast, around and on top of meat, fish or vegetables.

PROVENÇAL BREADCRUMBS WITH EXTRA FLAVOURS Try adding any of the following:

Grated orange or lemon peel: The peel adds zesty freshness. I sprinkle this on top of meat, salads, grilled and roast vegetables or fish. Very good on top of root vegetable soups too.

Anchovies: Mix chopped anchovies with the breadcrumbs to make a gloriously gutsy topping for grilled steaks and roast beef.

Dried porcini or sundried tomatoes: The intensity of the finely chopped dried mushrooms and tomatoes makes them a vegan version of the anchovies. Excellent on beef, even better on baked mushrooms and tomatoes.

Chopped fresh chilli: Give the breadcrumbs a little spice, to brighten up grilled peppers, squash, aubergines, courgettes and tomatoes. It's also a great way to make a skinless chicken breast shout a little louder.

Pumpkin seeds/sunflower seeds/chia seeds/basil seeds: These add an extra layer of crunch to the breadcrumbs, perfect to sprinkle over the top of any sort of leaf or vegetable salad. The seedy Provençal breadcrumbs are delicious over cooked sweet vegetables like carrots, parsnips and pumpkin.

PROVENÇAL BREADCRUMB COATING This is the least messy way of making a Provençal or any breadcrumb coating. First get a tray, put your meat, chicken, fish fillet or fishcake on it. Dust the (i.e.) fishcake with flour on both sides. Brush beaten egg generously over the top and sides of each fishcake. Pat half of the breadcrumbs over the top, then, using a fish slice, turn each cake over and brush with egg wash. Coat the tops and sides with the remaining breadcrumbs and press gently. (This also means that if you make fishcakes and they are a little soft, they don't break up as you coat them as they would if you needed to transfer them to separate dishes of flour, egg and breadcrumbs.)

Frying the breadcrumb-coated food briefly then finishing it in the oven works much better than simply frying. The interior gets time to cook or heat before the exterior burns.

Here are few good things to use as 'glue', in place of the beaten egg:

Grain mustard, good with pork

Dijon mustard, good with lamb, pork, chicken and most fish

Olive tapenade, good with most Mediterranean vegetables, meats and fish

Red curry paste (p.76), good with lamb, oily fish and chicken

Basil pistou (p.28), good with Mediterranean vegetables, halloumi or mozzarella cheese, meats and fish

TOPPING FOR CREAMY AND CHEESY GRATINS
Mix the breadcrumbs with grated Gruyère or Cheddar and use to top your cheesy or creamy gratin before you bake it. This works well with cauliflower cheese or macaroni cheese, for example.

TOPPING FOR BOILED BROCCOLI, CAULIFLOWER AND ASPARAGUS
Put 25g butter per person into a small pan. Heat until the butter browns lightly. Stir in 2 tbsp Provençal breadcrumbs and 2 tbsp roughly chopped boiled egg. Scatter this over the cooked vegetables.

BREADCRUMBS TO BIND MEATBALLS AND STUFFING
To make your meat go further and your meatballs or stuffing more tender and tastier, use a mixture of 2 parts mince and 1 part Provençal breadcrumbs.

BREADCRUMBS ON TOP OF ROAST TOMATOES
Cut tomatoes in half and slow-roast them for 90 minutes at 140°C/Gas 1. Brush them with olive oil, and cover the cut tops with Provençal breadcrumbs. Grill lightly until the crumbs are crisp.

CRUMBS, THAT'S A NICE MAYO
Stir Provençal breadcrumbs into mayonnaise. Add a few capers and chopped gherkins too if you have them.

Don Alfonso's aubergines

Don Alfonso was my boss during a wonderful sojourn in the south of Italy. During that long summer I practically lived on aubergines and tomatoes from Don Alfonso's 'farm', a glorious 2,000-tree olive grove woven with tomatoes, aubergines, courgettes, lemons, figs and basil, all overlooking the sea and Capri. We'd often eat this dish for staff dinner: it's a lot of untidy fun to prepare, but the divine taste and oozing cheese more than make up for the mess.

Get kids to join in. It's really a stacked-up crunchy aubergine pizza, and a good way to introduce younger kids to aubergines. Good to purée or chop and freeze for babies and toddlers.

Serves 2

Sides A crisp salad with lemon dressing

Prep/cooking time 45 mins

Active time 30 mins

. . . .

1 small, very firm aubergine

2½ tbsp extra virgin olive oil, plus extra to trickle

1 tbsp balsamic vinegar

2 very ripe large plum tomatoes

2 x 250g mozzarella cheeses, very well drained and dried (drained weight, each ball 125g)

16 large basil leaves

1 small egg

★ 50g Provençal breadcrumbs (p.148)

30g Parmesan cheese, freshly grated

Salt, caster sugar and cayenne pepper

1. Preheat your oven to 200°C/Gas 6, rack position top shelf.

2. Start with the aubergine. Cut the green top off. Cut the aubergine in half lengthways. With the flat side down, slice each half horizontally into 3 lengthways, making 6 slices. Line a baking sheet with a re-usable non-stick mat. Put the slices flat on the tray.

3. Get a small bowl. Add the extra virgin olive oil and balsamic vinegar. Season with salt, sugar and cayenne pepper. Brush the aubergine slices on both sides with two-thirds of this mixture. Bake in your preheated oven for 10 minutes. Take the aubergine slices out of the oven. Brush them with the remaining balsamic mixture. Leave the oven on.

4. While the aubergine bakes, slice each tomato into 4 lengthways. Put the slices onto a plate lined with kitchen paper. Slice each mozzarella into 4. Put the slices next to the tomatoes. Season both with salt and pepper.

5. Do all of the following work on the aubergine's baking tray. Put a slice of tomato at one end of each of 4 aubergine slices. Overlap each tomato slice with 2 basil leaves. Overlap the basil with a slice of mozzarella. Repeat this so that 4 of the aubergine slices are completely covered with tomato, basil and mozzarella.

6. Put 2 of the covered slices of aubergine on top of the other 2. Finally, put the remaining 2 'empty' aubergine slices on top and press down firmly so that the 3 layers stick together.

7. Get 2 small bowls. Beat the egg in the first. Mix the breadcrumbs and grated Parmesan in the second. Brush the beaten egg generously all over the aubergine sandwiches. Press the breadcrumb and Parmesan mixture over the tops and sides to make sure that they stick. If any crumbs fall off, push them back on.

8. Bake for 15 minutes until the crumbs are brown and crisp. I cut the finished aubergines in half for the photo so you could see how lovely they look inside, but you don't have to. Serve with a trickle of extra virgin olive oil.

No-meat chestnut 'meatballs' with tomato sauce

The Provençal breadcrumbs bind the chestnut purée to make an excellent base for a ball to rival mince for vegetarians and meat-eaters alike. (Chestnut purée has a multitude of uses from soup to pudding and should be on your magic tricks shelf.) You can make the balls vegan by leaving out the egg yolk, it just means they are more fragile.

Making this recipe with your kids, transforming ingredients from mixture to balls, is a great way to spend time together. Good to purée or chop and freeze for babies and toddlers.

Serves 2

Sides Pasta, giant couscous, polenta, quinoa, potatoes or bread

Prep/cooking time 35-40 mins

Active time 20 mins

....

1 medium onion (150-175g), peeled and finely chopped

2 tbsp extra virgin olive oil

200g tinned chopped tomatoes in juice

200ml vegetable stock or bouillon, fresh or made with powder/cube

100g chestnut purée

★ 75g Provençal breadcrumbs, plus 25g to sprinkle (p.148)

125g (½ pouch) ready-to-eat Puy lentils

1 large egg yolk

A little plain flour, for dusting your hands

Salt and freshly ground black pepper

1. Start with the tomato sauce. Get a medium-sized (24cm) shallow pan. Add the onion and extra virgin olive oil. Sweat over a low to medium heat for 6-7 minutes until the onion is soft. Add the tinned tomato and vegetable stock. Simmer gently while you make the chestnut balls.

2. Get a large bowl. Add the chestnut purée, 75g Provençal breadcrumbs, cooked lentils and the egg yolk. Mix together. Season to taste. Squeeze the mixture into 14 even-sized pieces. Dust your hands with flour. Roll the 14 pieces into balls between your palms.

3. Add the chestnut balls to the simmering sauce in a single layer. Brush the balls with the sauce. Simmer gently for 20 minutes, brushing the balls three times.

4. Sprinkle the 25g Provençal breadcrumbs over the top. Serve with something nice to soak up the last of the sauce.

Cook extra

This reheats very well and will also freeze, so make as much as you can!

Plaice with Provençal breadcrumb crust, chilli & lemon butter

There was a time when a herb crust on fish was the ultimate in sophistication for me. Nostalgia prompted me to give it a try for this book, and it is as wonderful as it ever was. In those days, herb-crusted fish was often served with a beurre blanc, so I needed a butter sauce with something sharp to really set it off, which both lemon and chilli do nicely. This recipe can also be cooked with hake, coley, gurnard or any other white fish.

This is a great way to introduce younger kids to both herbs and different fish. Leave out the chilli and it is good to purée or chop and freeze for babies and toddlers.

Serves 2

Sides Any grain, simmered potatoes, cauliflower

Prep/cooking time 25 mins

Active time 25 mins

. . . .

2 x 125g (or close) skinless plaice fillets

2 tsp Dijon mustard

★ 50g Provençal breadcrumbs (p.148)

200ml vegetable stock or bouillon, fresh or made with powder/cube

50g unsalted butter, diced

½ mild red chilli, de-seeded and finely chopped

Grated zest of ½ lemon and 2 tbsp juice

½ head broccoli, stalk peeled, cut in half again

Salt, sugar and cayenne pepper or piment d'Espelette

1. Preheat your oven to 200°C/Gas 6, rack position upper middle shelf. Boil your kettle. Fill a medium-sized (20cm) saucepan with the boiling water. Add salt. Put the saucepan onto your cooker. Put a colander in your sink.

2. Get a baking tray. Line it with a re-usable non-stick mat. Put the plaice fillets on the lined tray. Season both sides with salt and cayenne pepper. Brush the top and sides of each portion of plaice with 1 tsp Dijon mustard. Spread the Provençal breadcrumbs over both fillets and press them down gently.

3. Bake the plaice for 6-8 minutes. To check if the plaice is cooked, put the tip of a skewer or knife into the thickest part of the flesh, it should come out hot. If the plaice is ready before you are, turn off your oven, leave the door slightly ajar and it'll keep warm without overcooking for a few minutes.

4. While the plaice bakes, make the sauce. Get a medium-sized saucepan. Add the vegetable stock. Bring to the boil over a high heat and reduce by two-thirds. Turn the heat to low. Whisk in the butter bit by bit, followed by the chilli, the lemon zest and the lemon juice. Don't let the sauce boil again or it will separate. Season to taste with salt, sugar and cayenne pepper.

5. Boil the broccoli for 2-3 minutes until tender. Drain the cooked broccoli carefully in your colander.

6. Spoon the sauce onto your plates. Use a strong fish slice to put the plaice on one side and the boiled broccoli on the other.

Stuffed mushrooms with Provençal breadcrumbs

Large flat mushrooms are gutsy enough to be the basis for a main course, especially when they are combined with a pulse. Ready-cooked pulses are fabulous fast food and you can use their juices as stock. The wonderful Don Alfonso, my old boss in the south of Italy, makes a pasta dish with chickpeas and their cooking juices. He would serve it and say, 'This is better than meat' and this dish quite possibly is. If you fancy a simpler sauce, some melted butter with garlic and parsley would do nicely, as would the lemon butter (p.64).

If younger kids don't go for mushrooms, it tends to be the texture - just keep trying. The alcohol is cooked out in the sauce so this is good to purée or chop and freeze for babies and toddlers.

Serves 2

Sides Nothing is needed

Prep/cooking time
40-50 mins

Active time 30 mins

. . . .

6 medium-sized flat mushrooms

3 tbsp extra virgin olive oil

2 large garlic cloves, peeled and thinly sliced

1 medium onion (150-175g), peeled and thinly sliced

½ x 400g tin chickpeas, drained (keep the juices)

½ x 25g pack dried porcini mushrooms, soaked in 100ml hot water

200ml red wine (Cabernet Sauvignon is good)

1 tbsp dark soy sauce

½ tsp cornflour

★ 50g Provençal breadcrumbs (p.148)

Salt, freshly ground black pepper and caster sugar

1. Preheat your oven to 220°C/Gas 7, rack position upper middle shelf.

2. Start with the mushrooms. Take out their stalks, slice these finely and set aside to use in the gravy. Put the mushrooms, rounded-side down, onto a roasting tray. Brush with 2 tbsp of the extra virgin olive oil. Season with salt and pepper.

3. Roast the mushrooms for 5 minutes. Take them out of the oven and leave them on their tray. Turn the oven down to 200°C/Gas 6.

4. Get a medium-sized frying pan. Add the garlic, onion, 1 tbsp extra virgin olive oil and 1 tbsp water. Put the lid on. Sweat over a low to medium heat for 6-7 minutes until the onions soften. Take the lid off, add the drained chickpeas, turn up the heat and fry for 3 minutes until everything is golden.

5. Squeeze the now reconstituted porcini dry, saving the liquid for the sauce. Slice the porcini finely and add to the pan. Fry for 1 minute then transfer the chickpea mixture to a bowl.

6. Add the red wine and sliced mushroom stalks to the empty pan, bring to the boil and reduce by two-thirds. Add the soaking liquid from the porcini, the soy sauce and the chickpea juice.

7. Boil over a high heat to reduce by half. Dilute the cornflour in 1 tbsp water. Whisk it into the sauce. Bring back to the boil. Boil for 30 seconds. Take the pan off the heat. Season to taste with salt, black pepper and sugar.

8. While the wine reduces, put one-third of the chickpea mixture into a small food processor and blend to a smooth purée. Add 1-2 tbsp hot water if the mixture is too dry to purée. Stir this purée back into the rest of the chickpea mixture. Stir in half of the Provençal breadcrumbs. Season to taste. Stuff the mushrooms with the chickpea mixture. Put the rest of the Provençal breadcrumbs on top. Bake in your preheated oven for 10 minutes. Serve with the porcini sauce.

PIZZA BASES

I like my pizza with a thin and crisp base. If you prefer your base thick, like a loaf of warm bread with good things on top, go for it. The only 'right' way to eat your pizza is the way you like it best. The dough is rewarding to make, the intoxicating scent of yeast and olive oil giving you the energy to knead with abandon.

I've broken a few rules by using fast-action yeast so that you can just knead the dough together, let it rest, roll it and be ready to bake in 30 minutes. You don't have to make pizza in circles: a large rectangle - i.e. the biggest size that fits in your freezer or oven - is often more practical. From this same simple and speedy dough you can make a traditional pizza, you can vary the toppings, make pizza pie, Provençal stuffed fougasse, or a giant sandwich. Pizza is fun; more so, more satisfying and more delicious when you deliver your own.

Pizza is a magical way to get kids into cooking - a perfect adventure for their senses. When kids make pizza together, they encourage each other to try things, often for reasons that are more visual than nutritional, but inspiration to eat more variety can come from anywhere. It might be an introduction to olives because they make good eyes on a pizza face, or mushrooms because they make good ears. Start kids on a pizza-based vegetable discovery and their health and happiness will reap the rewards.

Makes 6 x 25cm pizza bases or 8-10 smaller ones

Storage Fridge 6-7 hours. Freezer 3 months

Prep time 30 mins

Active time 20 mins

....

1kg strong white bread flour, plus extra for dusting

4 x 7g sachets fast-action yeast

2 tsp caster sugar

4 tsp salt

580ml lukewarm water

4 tbsp extra virgin olive oil, plus 1-2 tbsp for brushing the paper

1. Get a large bowl. Add the flour, yeast, sugar and salt. Make a little well in the middle. Pour in the water and the extra virgin olive oil.

2. Mix with one hand until everything is well combined into a dough.

3. Transfer the dough to your worktop. Knead for 6-7 minutes until the dough is very smooth.

4. Separate the dough into 6 (or more or less if you want smaller or larger pizza) pieces. Put them onto a large floured plate or tray. Dust with flour. Cover with clingfilm. Put the dough into your fridge. Leave to rest for 20 minutes. This rest relaxes the dough and makes it possible to flatten it without the dough bouncing back at you.

5. Cut 6 x 28cm squares of greaseproof paper. Brush each square with extra virgin olive oil. Put a ball of dough onto a square of paper. Flatten the dough with your fingers into a 25cm circle, square or rectangle. Put a piece of oiled greaseproof paper on top then continue with the next one. Once you have done them all, stack them up on a plate so they are easier to carry.

How to store

Freeze the pizza bases. Once the dough is frozen, wrap the pizza bases individually in clingfilm. Your pizza bases are now ready to take from the freezer one by one. They take about 15-20 minutes to defrost in a warm kitchen.

PIZZA BASES
MAGIC IDEAS

I see endless opportunities when I look at my pizza bases. Not just an opportunity to put different toppings on tomato sauce, but to make different 'spreads' in place of the tomato sauce. One of my favourites is the soft, sweet onions that top pissaladière, Nice's anchovy- and olive-topped pizza that is one of the world's great street foods. Another is a rich cheesy mixture of mascarpone and Parmesan that I crave constantly and is delicious with any sort of sundried or semidried tomatoes, roasted peppers, squash, aubergine and courgettes, as well as cooked or cured hams and chorizo. These can all be encased in the pizza pie or the fougasse farci (the Provençal version of a stuffed pasty).

Unusually for me, I am very set in my ways about how I like to eat pizza with tomato, and I'm sure you'll already have your favourite toppings from pepperoni to pineapple - so here I want to explore the idea of a magical pizza playtime in other ways.

PIZZA WITH MASCARPONE AND PARMESAN SAUCE See the recipe for mascarpone sauce on p.174, and use it to top your pizza base instead of tomato sauce. Then add any of the following:

Roast aubergine seasoned with balsamic vinegar

Olives, anchovies and roast peppers (There are some very good tinned or bottled peppers available, I like Roquito pepper pearls on this one as well.)

Smoked salmon, lemon zest and dill

Garlic mushrooms Turn the mushrooms upside down. Put chopped garlic and rosemary inside them. Spread them evenly over the top of the pizza.

Sundried tomatoes, feta and rocket

PIZZA WITH SWEET AND STICKY ONIONS See the recipe for sweet and sticky onions on p.169, and spread it over your pizza base instead of tomato sauce. Then add any of the following:

Olives and anchovies

Chorizo and goat's cheese

Camembert and smoked bacon lardons

Raisins, pine nuts, rocket and feta cheese

Salami, green olives, halved baby plum tomatoes and basil

ALTERNATIVE STUFFING IDEAS FOR FOUGASSE Use the recipe on p.167, with the following stuffings instead:

Sunblush or sundried tomatoes in oil, halved tinned artichoke hearts, olives and basil

Sautéed mushrooms with lots of garlic, whole parsley leaves and cream cheese

Caramelised onion or onion chutney, orange zest and chunks of Camembert

Ricotta cheese mixed with ratatouille (p.112)

Sautéed spinach, smoked salmon and mascarpone cheese

ALTERNATIVE FILLING IDEAS FOR PIZZA PIES Use the recipe on p.170, and fill your pizza pie with any of the following:

 Spinach and feta filling: Soften onions and garlic in olive oil. Stir in spinach until it wilts. Add crumbled feta cheese. Add raisins to taste. Season with salt and za'atar, herbes de Provence or dried oregano.

Tomato, cream cheese and salmon filling: Start with a thick tomato sauce. Stir in cream cheese. Flake hot smoked salmon into it. Mix in sliced watercress.

Creamy bacon and lentil filling: Fry bacon lardons. Add sliced onion and garlic and cook to soften them. Stir in cooked lentils, mascarpone cheese and lots of freshly ground black pepper.

Ratatouille filling: Ratatouille (p.112) can be mixed with just about anything in a pizza pie - you can go salty with feta, creamy with goat's cheese, herby with pistou or earthy with Puy lentils. It's also great made meaty with smoked chicken, ham or bacon.

Memories of Sorrento pizza

The way I bake and eat pizza is the result of a summer working near Sorrento. Every Sunday after service we single cooks ate at a place where huge hams hung above tiny tables and huge men baked pizza by the metre. We'd eat a metre of the most magnificent Margherita; there was no other topping available and if we wanted the cured ham, we were ordered to only add it, cold, once the pizza was cooked.

The tomatoes want to kick and scream with flavour. The key is to leave them to sit in the salt for 20 minutes. This intensifies their taste and gets rid of the excess moisture that makes the pizza base soggy. The timing works well as you can make the topping while the fresh dough rests or the frozen dough defrosts.

Serves 2

Sides I have to have a balsamic and olive oil dressed green salad on the side when I eat pizza

Prep/cooking time 40–50 mins

Active time 15–20 mins

. . . .

600g ripest possible plum tomatoes

1 tsp salt

1 tsp caster sugar

¼ tsp cayenne pepper

★ 2 pizza bases (p.160)

2 x 250g mozzarella cheeses, extremely well drained and dried (drained weight, each ball 125g)

3 tbsp extra virgin olive oil, plus a little extra for trickling

6 tbsp sliced basil

1. Preheat your oven to 220°C/Gas 7, rack position upper middle shelf. Put a baking sheet onto the rack to heat it.

2. Start with the tomatoes. Cut out their cores. Cut them in half then chop the flesh into small (1.5cm) chunks. Put the chunks into a large bowl. Add the 1 tsp each of salt and sugar and the ¼ tsp cayenne pepper. Tip the mixture into a sieve, put the sieve over the top of the bowl you used for the tomatoes then leave to sit for 20 minutes.

3. Take the pizza bases out of the freezer. Put them onto a re-usable non-stick mat on a tray. Leave them to defrost.

4. While the tomatoes drain, squeeze the mozzarella balls to get rid of as much liquid as possible. Cut the mozzarella into 2cm dice. Pat dry with kitchen paper. Do not cover.

5. After 20 minutes, stir the tomatoes and shake off all the liquid you can. (This liquid is very nice to drink.) Transfer the chopped tomatoes to a bowl. Stir in the extra virgin olive oil and two-thirds of the basil.

6. Scatter the tomato mixture evenly over the pizza bases. Put the dried mozzarella dice evenly over the top.

7. Take the baking sheet out of the oven. Slide the pizzas with their mat onto it. Put them into the oven and bake for 15–20 minutes until golden and crisp.

8. Slide the pizzas from the baking sheet onto a chopping board. With one hand, hold the side of the pizza steady with a fish slice, with the other hand slide the mat out from underneath. Sprinkle the rest of the basil over the pizzas.

9. I serve my pizza on the chopping board with a trickle of extra virgin olive oil over the top.

Fougasse stuffed with chorizo, cheese & 'smoked' tomato

This is my Provençal pasty. The loaf's shape, in a very abstract way, is meant to resemble a head of wheat. You can speed it up by leaving out the slashes and simply covering the filling to make the circle of dough into a half circle. Smoked paprika is an excellent seasoning for tomatoes: by brushing it over the top of the dough I bring filling and casing closer together. These are very generous portions. If you have any left over, I can heartily recommend it toasted with cheese on top or doused with extra virgin olive oil the next day.

Serves 2 generously

Sides A crisp lettuce or vegetable salad is good. I like a beetroot and carrot coleslaw

Prep/cooking time 30–35 mins

Active time 20 mins

. . . .

★ 2 pizza bases (p.160)

3 medium-sized ripe tomatoes (300g), cut into 2cm dice

1 tbsp tomato purée

½ tsp smoked paprika, plus ¼ tsp

2 tsp chopped rosemary

120g chorizo, cut into 2cm dice

250g mascarpone cheese

60g Parmesan cheese, freshly grated

10 garlic cloves

1 tbsp extra virgin olive oil

2 tsp plain flour, for dusting

Salt, caster sugar, salt flakes and smoked paprika

1. Preheat your oven to 220°C/Gas 7, rack position upper middle shelf. Boil your kettle.

2. Take the pizza bases out of the freezer. Put them directly onto a large baking sheet lined with a re-usable non-stick mat. Leave them to defrost while you prepare the filling.

3. Get a large (24–26cm) frying pan. Put the diced tomatoes and tomato purée into it. Add ½ tsp smoked paprika. Fry over a medium heat for 3–4 minutes to dry the tomatoes out and intensify their flavour. Take the pan off the heat. Transfer the mixture to a bowl. Leave to cool for 3 minutes. Stir in the rosemary, chorizo, mascarpone and Parmesan. Season to taste with salt and sugar. Add more smoked paprika if you want.

4. While the tomatoes fry, fill a small (16–18cm) pan with boiling water from your kettle. Add the garlic cloves, and bring back to the boil. Simmer for 5 minutes. (Alternatively just microwave the cloves for 20 seconds.) Drain.

5. Spread the tomato filling over one half of each pizza base, leaving 4cm free at the edge. Fold the dough over and seal the edges well. (You can stop here if you like, for a simple pasty shape.) Turn the filled dough so that the join is at the bottom, and press down to make an oval-shaped loaf, like a fat baguette. Pinch the ends. Slice 5 lines through the dough in each loaf to the point that you can see the ingredients in the middle. Put a boiled garlic clove in each hole.

6. Sprinkle ⅛ tsp smoked paprika over each loaf. Brush each loaf with ½ tbsp extra virgin olive oil. Sprinkle each loaf lightly with salt flakes. Dust each loaf with 1 tsp flour. Bake the loaves in the preheated oven for 12–14 minutes until they are golden brown.

7. I like to slice the fougasse, squeeze the soft garlic out of its skin, and spread a bit over each slice.

Sticky onion, fig, sunblush tomato & Gorgonzola pizza

This is inspired by the great pissaladière from Nice. The onions are caramelised until they are soft, sticky, deeply savoury and naturally sweet. They love something salty like the olives to set their sweetness alight, and enjoy a creamy touch too, here I've added Gorgonzola to ooze irresistibly into them.

The topping but not the crust is good to purée or chop and freeze for babies and toddlers. I'm always pleasantly surprised at how often kids love olives.

Serves 2

Sides A crunchy salad

Prep/cooking time
   40-45 mins

Active time 25-30 mins

. . . .

★ 2 pizza bases (p.160)

850g small firm red and/or white onions, peeled and cut into 5mm slices

4 garlic cloves, peeled and finely sliced

2 tbsp extra virgin olive oil

1 tbsp water

¼ tsp salt

¼ tsp caster sugar

¼ tsp freshly ground black pepper

120g Gorgonzola or any soft blue cheese

80-100g figs (2 large or 3 small), cut into small wedges

12 sunblush tomatoes

20 black olives, pitted and halved

½ tsp herbes de Provence or dried oregano

Salt, freshly ground black pepper and caster sugar

1. Take the pizza bases out of the freezer. Put them onto a re-usable non-stick mat on a tray. Leave them to defrost while you prepare the topping.

2. Preheat your oven to 220°C/Gas 7, rack position upper middle shelf. Put a baking sheet onto the rack to heat it.

3. Get a medium to large (24-26cm) sauté or frying pan that you have a lid for. Or if you don't have a lid, use a plate. Add the onions, garlic, oil, water, and the ¼ tsp each of salt, sugar and pepper. Cover the pan. Put the pan onto a medium heat. Sweat the onions without browning for 8 minutes until they are soft but not mushy. Stir 2-3 times to make sure the onions don't stick.

4. Take off the lid. Turn the heat up to high. Stand over the onions, stirring frequently, for 5-10 minutes (the time varies according to the water content of the onions) until the onions are golden brown and most of their liquid has evaporated. Add more oil if they start to stick. When they're ready, there should be no water in the pan and the onions should be soft and sticky. Turn off the heat. If, as often happens, there is some sticky onion stuck to the bottom of the pan, put the lid back on for 2 minutes. This will sweat the stickiness off. Give the onions a good stir and the softened tasty bits on the bottom of the pan will mix together wonderfully with the rest. Season to taste.

5. Spread the onions across the top of the pizza bases. Break the Gorgonzola into small 1-2cm chunks over the top of the onions. Put the figs, sunblush tomatoes and olives evenly over the top. Push all of these toppings into the onion or they will burn. Sprinkle the herbes de Provence over the top.

6. Take the baking sheet out of your preheated oven, and slide the pizzas with their mat onto it. Put them into the oven and bake for 12-15 minutes until golden and crisp.

Pizza pie

This is what I bake if I fancy lots of filling because I can pack it full of enough goodies to balance having dough above and below. If you have your Magic Freezer well stocked, you could replace the filling with ratatouille (p.112) instead of the mixture below; mix the ratatouille with the oregano and ricotta and you're away.

I've found pies to be a great hit with kids: they could have even more fun and make their own individual ones. The filling but not the cooked dough is good to purée or chop and freeze for babies and toddlers.

Serves 4-6

Sides A green salad

Prep/cooking time
50-55 mins

Active time 25-30 mins

. . . .

★ 2 pizza bases (p.160)

1 large red pepper and
1 large orange pepper

2 medium-sized onions
(150-175g each), peeled
and thinly sliced

4 garlic cloves, peeled and
thinly sliced

5 tbsp extra virgin olive oil

1 bunch or bag rocket
(80-100g), cut into
3cm slices

80g spinach, cut into
3cm slices

4 tbsp sliced oregano or
marjoram (or 2 tbsp dried)

250g ricotta cheese

50g fresh or dried
breadcrumbs, or Provençal
breadcrumbs (p.148)

2 tbsp freshly grated
Parmesan cheese

Plain flour, for dusting

Salt, freshly ground black
pepper and salt flakes

1. Preheat your oven to 220°C/Gas 7, rack position upper middle shelf.

2. Take 2 pizza bases out of the freezer. Put them onto an oven tray lined with a re-usable non-stick mat. Leave them to defrost.

3. Next, make the filling. Cut the 2 peppers in half lengthways. Take out the seeds. Cut the halves in half again, then cut the quarters widthways into thin (5mm) slices.

4. Get a large shallow pan. Add the peppers, sliced onions, sliced garlic, 3 tbsp of the extra virgin olive oil and a generous pinch of salt. Put a lid on the pan. Sweat over a medium heat for 10 minutes until the onions and peppers are soft. Raise the heat to high, remove the lid and fry for 3-4 minutes, stirring frequently until they catch and brown a little in the pan.

5. Add the rocket and spinach then stir for 30 seconds until they wilt.

6. Take the pan off the heat. Add the oregano. Stir in the ricotta, just enough to break it up. Season to taste with salt and pepper.

7. With a small knife, mark a 22cm circle inside one circle of dough, being careful not to cut all the way through. I use a plate to do this. Sprinkle the breadcrumbs over this circle.

8. Spoon the filling over the top of the marked circle.

9. Wet the edges of the dough. Lay the second circle of dough over the top of the filling. Press the edges down well so that they stick together. Crimp the edges with a fork. Brush with 2 tbsp extra virgin olive oil. Sprinkle the Parmesan and salt flakes over the top. Lightly dust with flour.

10. Bake for 15-20 minutes in your preheated oven or until the pie is golden brown. Eat hot, warm or at kitchen temperature.

PANCAKES

Whisking, tossing, flipping, then smothering pancakes with glorious toppings and eating them greedily is all part of the fun. This is easily the best of the half dozen pancake recipes I tried. My beautiful baker friend, Bertinet, taught me the trick with the pan and the half potato.

Make pancakes when you've got plenty of time to practice flipping, it's the best way to turn them over. Stock up, pancakes are one of the most versatile things that you can have in your Magic Freezer.

Makes 20 x 20cm pancakes

Storage Fridge 3 days.
Freezer 3 months

Prep/cooking time
35-45 mins (you will get faster as you go)

Active time 35-45 mins

. . . .

3 large eggs

675ml full-fat milk

110g butter, melted, plus extra for frying

1½ tbsp caster sugar, plus extra (optional) for sprinkling

¾ tsp salt

375g plain flour

1 small potato, cut in half (optional)

1. Get a large bowl. Add the eggs, milk, melted butter, sugar and salt. Whisk together. Whisk in half the flour. Once the flour is well mixed in, add the other half and keep whisking until the batter is totally smooth. Cover the batter with clingfilm. Leave it next to your cooker if you're using the batter within an hour, or in the fridge if you're leaving it longer.

2. The best way to know how much to use for each pancake is to find a ladle and do a tester with the first one. I use a ladle that makes a perfect pancake when it's half full. Just over 3 tbsp for a 20cm pan is about right.

3. Get your 20cm non-stick frying pan hot then turn the heat down to medium. The pan needs to be lightly coated with but not swimming in fat. The easiest way I've found is to dip the cut face of a halved potato into melted butter and wipe the pan with it. Pour in the portion of batter. Swirl it around from side to side to get the pan's base evenly coated with batter. Fry for 30-45 seconds until the pancake is golden brown. (If you're not sure, lift the edge of the pancake with a palette knife and have a peek.) Turn the pancake then fry on the other side for 10 seconds. The second side cooks just enough so that it won't stick to the other pancakes in the pile; fry for too long and the pancakes become hard and crisp.

4. Slide the pancake onto a plate. If you want to keep the pancakes hot, put the plate over a pot of simmering water and cover it with foil.

5. If I am making sweet pancakes, I sprinkle a little sugar over each before putting the next one on top.

How to store

Freeze the pancakes that you are not going to eat within a few days between layers of greaseproof paper. Once they are frozen hard you can wrap them individually, or in little groups of 2 or 4. I strongly recommend storing the pancakes on a plastic plate, as they become very brittle when they are frozen and can break easily.

PANCAKES
MAGIC IDEAS

Pancakes can be whatever you want them to be, whenever you feel like eating them. If you have a pile of pancakes in the freezer you've always got an option for a main course, dessert, snack or a naughty treat. Because they're so thin, they defrost in a flash and they've become one of my favourite midnight feasts: I love a late-night pancake rolled up with ham and cheese then microwaved to a divine molten mess.

SALMON AND CREAM CHEESE PANCAKES
Warm your pancakes in the microwave for 30 seconds or so on high. Mix crème fraîche or mascarpone cheese with chopped fresh dill. Season with plenty of black pepper, spread the cream across the pancakes and top with slices of smoked salmon.

SUNBLUSH TOMATO AND GOAT'S CHEESE PANCAKE
Warm your pancakes and spread them with basil pistou (p.28). Crumble over some fresh goat's cheese and dot with sunblush or rehydrated sundried tomatoes. Either roll the pancakes up and eat them immediately or bake for 10–15 minutes at 200°C/Gas 6 until the cheese is golden for a pancake pizza.

ROLLED PANCAKES
Cheese sauce (p.40) is the classic. Mix it with almost any cooked vegetable or meat, roll it inside your pancakes, heat them in the microwave (the timing will vary depending on what you have stuffed them with), then grill them golden with grated cheese on top. Ratatouille (p.112) can be rolled hot or cold into pancakes on its own, or with feta, mozzarella, sunblush or sundried tomatoes. I love a hot ratatouille pancake with a fried egg on top.

A QUICK MASCARPONE 'SAUCE'
This 'sauce' goes with pretty much everything and is irresistible. Mix 2 parts mascarpone cheese together with 1 part grated Parmesan and season with salt and freshly ground black pepper. Add ham, cooked leeks, broccoli, spinach, kale, mushrooms, chestnuts, herbs, cooked chicken, or mixtures of these ideas. Spread the sauce and vegetables over half of each pancake, then fold the other half over the top to make a half-moon shape. Heat the pancakes in your microwave: the time will vary depending on what you have stuffed them with.

SAVOURY PANCAKE SPREADS Spread basil pistou (p.28) and tomato chilli relish (p.124) over warm pancakes and eat as is, or top with feta, mozzarella, cured/cooked/smoked ham, smoked salmon, rocket, tomatoes, roast peppers, or mixtures of these ideas.

HOT LEMON BUTTER AND SUGAR Melt lemon butter (p.64) and spoon it over the top of pancakes. Sprinkle granulated sugar or herb or citrus sugar (p.259) over the top.

ALMOND CREAM TART Spread almond cream (p.184) thickly over a pancake. Scatter flaked almonds over the top. Dust with icing sugar. Bake for 10–12 minutes at 200°C/Gas 6.

BANANA AND DULCE DE LECHE PANCAKES For a luscious treat, peel a couple of bananas and slice them thickly. Smear the bananas with dulce de leche, squeeze over the juice of a lime or lemon and bake them for 10 minutes at 200°C/Gas 6. Spread your pancakes with more dulce de leche and once the bananas are cooked put them onto the pancakes then roll them up. For a simpler but equally delicious version, warm the pancakes, spread them with dulce de leche and roll them around raw bananas. Serve with cream or ice cream.

TEN-MINUTE PANCAKE TART Put a pancake on a re-usable non-stick mat on a baking tray. Sprinkle on plenty of caster sugar and ground cinnamon. Peel a Granny Smith apple and slice it as thinly as you can. Fan it around the pancake as prettily as possible in a single layer. Put more sugar and cinnamon over the top along with a good knob of butter. Bake at 200°C/Gas 6 for 10 minutes or until golden. Serve with some crème fraîche or vanilla ice cream, or both.

My 'huevos rancheros' pancakes

'Huevos rancheros' means 'rancher's eggs'. I've never actually been to a ranch, but the idea of poaching eggs in tomato and pepper sauce is a beauty. At different times I add beluga lentils, bacon, sausages or chorizo to this. The pancakes turn it into a full meal, great for dinner, breakfast or lunch, but somehow most at home for brunch. The Roquitos perk up the eggs enormously and the sauce just kicks and screams with flavour. If you can't get Roquitos, add chilli for spice and baby plum tomatoes for extra juiciness.

Lay off the spice a little and this is great to purée or chop and freeze for babies and toddlers.

Serves 2

Sides Nothing is needed

Prep/cooking time 25 mins

Active time 25 mins

. . . .

1 medium onion (150g), peeled and thinly sliced

½ yellow pepper, de-seeded and thinly sliced

3 tbsp extra virgin olive oil

4 tbsp water

1 x 400g tin best-quality chopped tomatoes in juice

★ 4 pancakes (p.172)

2 large eggs

½ ripe avocado, peeled

2 tbsp chopped chives

2 tbsp Roquito pearls, or 1 fresh red chilli, de-seeded and finely diced

Salt, chilli powder and caster sugar

1. Preheat your oven to 200°C/Gas 6, rack position upper middle shelf.

2. Start with the sauce. Get a medium to large (24-26cm) shallow, ovenproof frying pan. Add the onion, yellow pepper, 2 tbsp extra virgin olive oil and the water. Cover the pan. Sweat over a high heat, stirring occasionally, for 8 minutes until the onions and peppers are soft. Add the tinned tomatoes, bring to the boil, then turn the heat down to medium. Simmer for 5 minutes, stirring 3 or 4 times so that it doesn't catch on the bottom of the pan. Season to taste with salt, some sugar to balance the acidity of the tomatoes, and as much chilli powder as you like.

3. Fold the pancakes in quarters. Slide them into the sauce around the edges of the frying pan. Brush the pancakes all over with the sauce.

4. Break the eggs into the sauce. Put the pan into the oven for 10 minutes for eggs that are barely set.

5. Cut the avocado into 2cm chunks. Put the chunks into a shallow bowl and gently mix them with a pinch of salt, the chives, Roquito pearls (or diced chilli) and 1 tbsp extra virgin olive oil.

6. Once the eggs are cooked, scatter the avocado mixture over the top. Serve straight from the pan.

Cook extra

The onion, pepper and tomato mixture will keep for a couple of days in the fridge and can be frozen. It's a good one to add to your Magic Freezer.

Pancake, spinach, tomato & smoked salmon lasagne

This is a dish that illustrates how versatile pancakes can be. The lasagne keeps in the fridge for a couple of days and freezes brilliantly, so get into the spirit of the Magic Fridge and make more than you need. For a meaty version you could replace the tomato sauce with a savoury mince, or mix chopped ham into the cheese sauce. A microwave is best for this 'bake' sort of recipe: all you need to do is heat it through before you grill it to brown the top. Make the lasagne in a 22-24cm round or 25 x 20cm rectangular ovenproof dish.

It's a great recipe to get kids to assemble. Good to purée or chop and freeze for babies and toddlers.

Serves 4

Sides A crisp salad is nice

Prep/cooking time 30-50 mins (depending on whether you microwave or bake)

Active time 20 mins

. . . .

1 medium-sized onion (150-175g), peeled and finely chopped

4 garlic cloves, peeled and finely chopped

2 tbsp extra virgin olive oil

2 x 400g tins chopped tomatoes in juice

6 tbsp sliced basil

1 tbsp vegetable oil

360g spinach leaves (2 typical supermarket packets), washed

375g mascarpone cheese

175g Cheddar cheese, grated, plus 50g for the top

6 pancakes (p.172)

120g smoked salmon

Salt, freshly ground black pepper and freshly grated nutmeg

1. Preheat your oven to 190°C/Gas 5, rack position middle shelf.

2. Start with the tomato sauce. Get a medium-sized saucepan (20cm). Add the onion, garlic and extra virgin olive oil. Put a lid on and sweat for 6-8 minutes over a medium heat until the onions are soft but not brown. Add the tinned tomatoes. Simmer briskly for 10 minutes, stirring at least 4 times, until almost all of the liquid has evaporated and you have a thick pulp. Take the pan off the heat. Season to taste. Stir in the sliced basil. Leave the sauce in the pan until you need it.

3. While the tomatoes simmer, get a large pan. Add the vegetable oil and get it really hot. Add the spinach. Stir-fry over a high heat for 1 minute or until the leaves are barely wilted. Season with salt, pepper and nutmeg, and transfer to a plate.

4. To make the cheese sauce, mix the mascarpone and 175g grated Cheddar together. Season to taste.

5. To make the lasagne, put a layer of 2 pancakes, overlapping, in the bottom of your dish. Cover with the tomato sauce. Cover the tomato sauce with 2 more pancakes. Spread the wilted spinach over the pancakes. Spread the smoked salmon over the top. Cover with 2 more pancakes. Spread the cheese sauce over the top. Sprinkle the 50g grated cheddar over the top of that.

6. Bake the pancake lasagne in your preheated oven for 20-25 minutes. (Alternatively heat it in the microwave for 4-5 minutes. Put the dish under a hot grill for 2-3 minutes until the cheese is evenly golden.)

7. Serve piping hot.

Passionfruit & citrus pancakes with lemon mascarpone

This pancake perks up any part of any day. The aroma of the syrupy sauce while it simmers is delightfully tropical, and the way the sauce soaks into the pancakes then moistens the mascarpone is truly decadent. If you want a cream-free fruity pancake, leave out the mascarpone.

Serves 2

Prep/cooking time 25 mins

Active time 25 mins

. . . .

1 red grapefruit

1 orange

2 passionfruit

100ml orange juice (from a carton is fine)

75g caster sugar

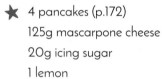 4 pancakes (p.172)

125g mascarpone cheese

20g icing sugar

1 lemon

1. First make the sauce. Get a medium-sized (20cm) shallow pan. Use a zester to cut the zest from the grapefruit and orange directly into the pan.

2. Cut the top and bottom off the grapefruit and orange so that they sit flat on your chopping board. Cut the peel off in strips, being sure to cut away all the white pith. Put a sieve over the shallow pan. Hold 1 citrus fruit at a time over the sieve then cut out each segment of flesh between the white membranes. Once you have cut out all the segments, squeeze the juice from the membranes into the shallow pan through the sieve. Transfer the citrus segments from the sieve into a bowl.

3. Cut the passionfruit in half. Scoop the seeds into the pan with the citrus zest and grapefruit juice. Add the orange juice and sugar. Bring this mixture to the boil and boil over a medium heat until it has reduced by two-thirds and is sticky and thick. (The sauce at this stage should be the same consistency as maple syrup; as it cools it will be closer to the consistency of jam.)

4. Fold the pancakes into quarters. Add them to the pan. Take the pan off the heat. Turn the pancakes in the pan so that they are completely coated with the sauce. Scatter the citrus segments over the top.

5. Get a small bowl. Add the mascarpone and icing sugar. Grate the lemon zest over the top. Whisk together.

6. Serve the pancakes, citrus segments and sauce with the lemon mascarpone.

Fig & chestnut pancake tart

I first came across the idea of using pancakes instead of pastry bases at the famed Auberge de la Mole, a restaurant near our old cookery school in Provence. They made a caramelised apple version of this to serve as a pre-dessert before a serve-yourself feast of crème caramel, chocolate mousse, pears in crème de Cassis and prunes in Armagnac. Fig and chestnuts are a mix from the magnificent month of September when they cross paths in Provence; in England's September the figs can be replaced with wild blackberries.

You will have some chestnut cream left over; you can use it in anything from the almond cream chapter (p.184).

Serves 2

Prep/cooking time 30 mins

Active time 20 mins

. . . .

180-200g (depending on packet size) cooked chestnuts

150g icing sugar, plus extra for dusting

150g unsalted butter, softened, plus 30g for brushing

1 large egg yolk

2 pancakes (p.172)

3 ripe figs

2 heaped tbsp apricot, raspberry or blackberry jam

2 tbsp water

4 tbsp or more crème fraîche (I like lots)

1. Preheat your oven to 200°C/Gas 6, rack position upper middle shelf.

2. Start with the chestnut cream. Separate the 3 biggest and prettiest chestnuts and leave them on your chopping board for later. Set up your food processor. Put the rest of the chestnuts in the bowl. Blend them to powder. Add the icing sugar, 150g butter and the egg yolk. Blend again until you have a very smooth cream. Let this take 2 minutes: the longer the cream blends, the lighter it becomes.

3. Line a small baking sheet with a re-usable non-stick mat. Put the 2 pancakes onto it. Put 80g of the chestnut cream onto each pancake. (Store the rest for another use, like a chestnut croissant in the style of the almond one on p.193.) Spread the chestnut cream almost to the edge of the pancakes.

4. Cut the 3 chestnuts you set aside into quarters. Push 6 quarters into the cream on each pancake tart.

5. Cut 1 of the figs in half. Put the halves, cut-face up, in the middle of the tarts. Cut the other 2 figs into 6 wedges. Put the 6 wedges between the 6 chestnut quarters.

6. Melt the 30g butter, and brush it over the figs. Dust the tarts generously with icing sugar.

7. Bake the tarts in the preheated oven for 12-15 minutes until they are light brown on top and very dark brown around the edges.

8. Put the jam and water together in a small cup or pan. Warm them through just enough to melt the jam. Brush the melted jam over the top of the tart to glaze the surface.

9. Serve with the crème fraîche.

Cook extra

I love these a day or so later for breakfast, hot or cold. So make at least one more than you need.

ALMOND CREAM

This is the mixture also known as frangipane, which may be familiar to you from almond croissants. Almond cream is made with butter rather than cream, but has a creamy texture: when it is baked it can go golden crisp on top and gloriously gooey underneath. Almond essence often gets added to it which, for me, completely destroys the cream with its synthetic taste. You can make the almond cream by hand, or just throw everything into the food processor for a minute. For a grown-up treat, add a few tablespoons of rum, brandy or amaretto. I often make the 'frangipane' with chestnuts instead of almonds.

You can make almond cream in a food processor, but my boys love stirring the butter smooth by hand and sieving the icing sugar, clouds of it filling the kitchen. It's a completely unnecessary process, but my goodness it's fun!

Makes Approx. 1.3kg

Storage Fridge 2 weeks.
Freezer 3 months

Prep/cooking time 10 mins

Active time 10 mins

. . . .

400g soft unsalted butter

400g icing sugar

4 large egg yolks

400g ground almonds

1. Get a large bowl. Add the butter and icing sugar. Mix together with a wooden spoon until the two are well combined and pale yellow in colour.

2. Stir in the egg yolks. Don't worry if it looks separated, this'll sort itself out when you add the ground almonds.

3. Add the ground almonds. Stir until they are well blended in.

4. Alternatively, put everything into your food processor and then blend until it is well combined and pale in colour. Do not try to make more than this amount in a domestic food processor – it'll be too hard on the motor.

How to store

Store in very clean airtight containers. I upcycle plastic takeaway containers with tight-fitting lids to store my almond cream in. A great upside to these is that they are microwavable and stackable. Store the cream in your containers in amounts that you are likely to use for the following recipes (180g for the almond croissants, 275g for the rhubarb pie, etc.). Do not touch the almond cream with your fingers. Cover the containers tightly. Refrigerate and/or freeze.

ALMOND CREAM
MAGIC IDEAS

Almond cream can be baked on its own as cookies, in a tart, in fruit, on toast, on pancakes and more. I'm still discovering new ways of using it 20 years on from my first batch; the almond and chocolate bread and butter pudding is my latest trick.

ALMOND AND BERRY BAKES If you have some frozen berries in your freezer and almond cream in your Magic Fridge, then you've got an almost instant dessert. Spread the fruit out in a single layer in an ovenproof dish. Add caster sugar to taste. Smooth almond cream over the top in a 4-5cm layer. Sprinkle with flaked almonds, dust with icing sugar and then bake at 190°C/Gas 5 for 15-20 minutes until golden.

BAKED APPLES WITH ALMOND FILLING Cut an apple in half. Microwave the halves until soft (this usually takes 3-4 minutes, covered, in my microwave). Be careful that they don't explode. Leave to cool for 4-5 minutes, they'll be volcanically hot. Scoop out the flesh and mix it to a purée with caster sugar to taste. Put the purée back into the skin. Top it with enough almond cream to fill the skin and sprinkle with flaked almonds. Dust with icing sugar and then bake for 12-14 minutes at 200°C/Gas 6 until golden.

BAKED ALMOND FRENCH TOAST Soak 2 thick slices of brioche first in 100ml double cream then in a beaten egg mixed with 2 tbsp caster sugar. Spread almond cream over the top and bake at 200°C/Gas 6 for 12-15 minutes until golden.

ALMOND AND CHOCOLATE BREAD AND BUTTER PUDDING Adapt your favourite bread and butter pudding by doing the following. Use almond cream mixed with cocoa powder instead of the butter to spread onto the bread. Scatter chunks of dark chocolate over the bread then pour over the custard and bake until golden.

TARTS GALORE Filo pastry, feuille de brique, puff pastry and short sweet pastry are all good to bake almond cream on. You can make the simplest of tarts by just spreading the almond cream over a puff or short sweet pastry rectangle. Or go one step further, spread the cream over the rectangle and then push halves of roast or tinned pears, apricots or fresh figs into it. Bake for 12-15 minutes at 200°C/Gas 6.

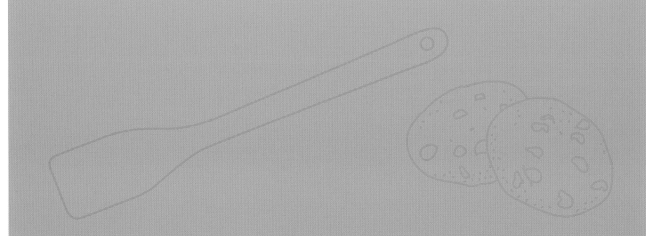

CHEWY ALMOND CREAM COOKIES

Use a spoon or piping bag to make cookie-sized circles of almond cream on a reusable non-stick mat. Then you can add chocolate chips, orange or lemon zest, you can put whole almonds in the middle, or scatter flaked almonds on top. Bake for 10-12 minutes on your middle shelf at 200°C/Gas 6, then cool to harden a little for 2-3 minutes before taking them off the mat. The cookies flatten out then become crunchy around the edges and moreishly chewy in the middle. Why not bake big flat ones and eat them hot with vanilla ice cream melting over the top!

PANCAKE, ALMOND AND RASPBERRY TART

Spread a 1.5cm deep layer of almond cream across a pancake (p.172) on a re-usable non-stick mat. Put 1 tsp raspberry jam (p220) in the middle. Dot 5 tsp jam around the outside. Sprinkle flaked almonds over the almond cream. Dust with icing sugar then bake for 15 minutes at 200°C/Gas 6 until golden.

PANCAKE ALMOND TARTS WITH TINNED APRICOTS

Spread a 1.5cm layer of almond cream across a pancake (p.172) on a re-usable non-stick mat. Put 5 apricot halves on top. Dust with icing sugar then bake for 15 minutes at 200°C/Gas 6 until golden. Melt 2 tbsp apricot jam then brush it over the apricots to glaze them.

PANCAKE AND ALMOND PIE

Spread a 1.5cm layer of almond cream across 2 pancakes (p.172) on a re-usable non-stick mat. Put 3 tbsp jam (p.220) in the middle of 1 pancake and put 6 small tinned pear halves pushed tightly together over the top of the almond cream and jam. Grate 25g dark chocolate over the pears. Put the second pancake spread with almond cream over the top, cream-side up, and press the edges over the pears. Scatter enough flaked almonds to cover the whole thing, dust with icing sugar, then bake at 200°C/Gas 6 for 15-17 minutes.

Baked apricots with almond cream & jam

Almonds and apricots have a natural affinity, perhaps because the apricot stone is called 'l'amande d'abricot' in French. In this recipe, I've effectively transformed the apricot halves into a pie base, the place where the 'apricot almond' once was provides the space for the almond cream to go. I used tinned apricots as I had them to hand, and they are delicious with the almond cream. You can replace them with fresh apricots, peaches, nectarines or plums, but you'll need to roast the fruit first to soften the flesh before you stuff it.

Stuffing the apricots with the almond cream is a great job for kids. They can even make each apricot into a hedgehog with flaked almonds in place of the pistachios on top of the almond cream.

Serves 2
Prep/cooking time 20 mins
Active time 20 mins

. . . .

8 (10 if they are very small) tinned apricot halves in syrup

120g almond cream (p.184)

2 heaped tbsp roughly chopped pistachio nuts

2 heaped tbsp dried cranberries

2 tsp icing sugar

3 tbsp apricot jam

3 tbsp syrup from the apricots

2 balls vanilla ice cream

1. Preheat your oven to 200°C/Gas 6, rack position middle shelf.

2. Line a baking sheet with a re-usable non-stick mat.

3. Put the apricot halves on the mat with the hole where the stone would have been facing up.

4. Cover each apricot half with an eighth (or tenth, depending on the size of the apricots) of the almond cream. Smooth the surface of the almond cream so that it is flat. Sprinkle half the pistachios and cranberries over the top. Pat them onto the cream so that they stick. Dust the filled apricots generously with icing sugar.

5. Bake in your preheated oven for 12 minutes, or until the tops are golden.

6. While the apricots bake, get a small (16-18cm) pan or bowl. Add the apricot jam and the measured syrup from the tinned apricots. Melt them together over a medium heat on your cooker or in your microwave. Stir well to combine the two: the texture needs to be saucy enough to thickly coat the back of a spoon. Stir in the second half of the pistachios and cranberries.

7. Serve the baked apricots with the sauce and the vanilla ice cream.

Cook extra

These apricots are like fruit-based mini almond croissants. I like them cold, even fridge cold, which is really unusual for me. Bake plenty of extras and have them for breakfast the next day.

Rhubarb, strawberry jam & almond pie

Almond, rhubarb and strawberry are an enchanting threesome of soft, tart and sweet. This pie is carefully designed not to need a tart tin: you put your pastry onto the baking sheet, pop everything on top, fold the edges up and bake away cheerfully. To make the pie even quicker to prepare, you can use shop-bought rhubarb compote. The pie will happily keep for two days.

Serves 6

Prep/cooking time 1¼ hours

Active time 40 mins

· ·

1 x 320g packet pre-rolled shortcrust pastry (35 x 23cm)

400g rhubarb, cleaned then cut into 7cm sticks on an angle (keep the trimmings)

150g caster sugar

5 tbsp water

1½ tsp cornflour

150g strawberry (or raspberry, p.220) jam

★ 275g almond cream (p.184), at kitchen temperature

1 egg yolk, mixed with 1 tbsp water, to glaze

50g flaked almonds

2 tbsp icing sugar

Clotted cream, to serve

1. Preheat your oven to 200°C/Gas 6, rack position middle shelf.

2. Boil your kettle. Take the pastry out of the fridge.

3. Start with the rhubarb. Get a large (24-30cm) shallow saucepan. Add the rhubarb (including the trimmings), sugar and 4 tbsp of water. Slowly bring to the boil. Put the lid on. Turn the heat down to low and gently poach the rhubarb for 3-4 minutes, turning it halfway through until the sticks are not quite soft and still holding their shape. Use a slotted spoon to gently transfer the 12 prettiest pink pieces of rhubarb to a plate. Turn the heat up to high and boil the remaining rhubarb, stirring for 5 minutes until the rhubarb becomes thick and jammy. Take the pan off the heat.

4. Dissolve the cornflour in 1 tbsp water. Stir the diluted cornflour into the rhubarb mush. Put the pan back on a high heat and boil for a further minute, stirring continually until the rhubarb mixture comes away from the side of the pan. Take the pan off the heat. Stir in the strawberry jam. Leave to cool.

5. Line a baking sheet with a re-usable non-stick mat. Unroll the pastry and put it on top.

6. Mark a 30 x 16cm rectangle in the middle of the pastry. Next, use a palette knife dipped in hot water to spread the rhubarb mixture over the marked rectangle. Make sure the almond cream is the texture of soft butter. If not, soften it a little in your microwave. Spread the almond cream over the top of the rhubarb mixture. Put the reserved 12 rhubarb sticks at even intervals over the top.

7. Turn the sides of the pastry over the top of the filling to make a 5cm border: this ensures the filling doesn't spill over the outsides.

8. Brush the pastry all over with the beaten egg yolk. Scatter the flaked almonds between the pieces of rhubarb and around the pastry. Press the almonds onto the glazed pastry so that they stick. Dust with the icing sugar. If any icing sugar spills over the sides onto the baking sheet, wipe it off as it will caramelise and burn as the pie cooks. Bake for 30-35 minutes in your preheated oven until the pie is golden all over. Serve with clotted cream.

The ultimate almond croissant

Almond croissants have become a mass-market victim of their own popularity. Truly great croissants are gnarly, misshapen, crunchy, creamy, delicious rejects, not the sad synthetic-tasting pastries we too often see. Almond croissants were invented as a way of using up old, dry croissants from the day before. These are soaked in syrup, filled and topped with almond cream, flaked almonds and icing sugar, then baked so that the outsides caramelise onto your baking tray. You agonisingly let them sit just long enough for this to harden, then you eat from sweet, crunchy edges through to soft, creamy centre. The Magic Fridge means that you can do this at home. You'll soon be buying croissants to let them go old on purpose.

The almond croissants will keep for a day or so once they are baked. Or make them up and freeze them unbaked.

Serves 2

Prep/cooking time
25–30 mins

Active time 15 mins

. . . .

200g caster sugar

200ml water

2 croissants, preferably
1–4 days old

★ 180g almond cream (p.184)

4 tbsp flaked almonds

2 tsp icing sugar

2 balls vanilla ice cream

1. Preheat your oven to 220°C/Gas 7, rack position middle shelf.

2. Line a baking sheet that has a lip with a re-usable non-stick mat and put it next to your cooker.

3. Get a small (16–18cm) shallow pan. Add the sugar and the water. Bring to the boil, and boil for 1 minute to dissolve the sugar completely. Take the pan off the heat.

4. Use a serrated knife to cut the croissants in half through the middle.

5. Put the croissant halves (two at a time) cut-side down, into the syrup. Leave them for 45 seconds. Turn the croissant halves. Leave them for 45 seconds. Lift the croissant halves with a fish slice, drain them a little then transfer them to your lined baking sheet with the cut sides facing up. You will have some syrup left over. Strain this and keep it in the fridge for another time.

6. Spread 50g almond cream across the bottom half of each croissant. Put the upper halves on top.

7. Spread 40g of almond cream all over the top of each croissant. Scatter the flaked almonds over the almond cream. Press them down lightly. Dust everything generously with the icing sugar.

8. Bake the croissants in your preheated oven for 10–12 minutes until they are golden. Take them out of the oven and leave them to sit for 2–3 minutes to harden a little.

9. Eat the croissants hot with the vanilla ice cream.

Peach & almond gratin with basil sugar

This recipe is a tremendous way of using up pears, apples, peaches, figs, grapes or nectarines that are past their best in your fruit bowl. It's not really a gratin because you don't actually gratinate it. But I couldn't think of anything else to call it, and like a gratin, the top goes wonderfully golden and crisp, so the name will do very nicely. You can make the gratin in 1 large or 4 individual ovenproof dishes.

Serves 4

Prep/cooking time 40 mins

Active time 20 mins

. . . .

4 large ripe peaches
  or nectarines

2 tbsp runny honey, plus
  extra if needed

2 tbsp orange juice (or
  apricot nectar, brandy
  or Grand Marnier)

★ 250g almond cream (p.184)

30g flaked almonds

1 tbsp icing sugar

4 tbsp basil leaves

Grated zest of ½ lemon

2 tbsp granulated sugar

4 tbsp crème fraîche
  (preferably Isigny), to serve

1. Preheat your oven to 190°C/Gas 5, rack position upper middle shelf.

2. Cut the peaches in half then give them a little twist to separate the halves. Take out and throw away the stones. Lay the peach halves, skin-side up, in your ovenproof dish. Drizzle the honey over the peaches. Pour over the orange juice. Depending on how ripe your peaches are, bake them for 10-15 minutes until they are soft. Taste one at this stage as stone fruits can get more acidic when they're cooked; add a little more honey if you want to. You can skip all of this and use bottled or tinned peaches.

3. Once the peaches are cooked, spread the almond cream over the top of them. Smooth the surface with a palette knife and don't worry if it's not too even, it'll be fine once it's cooked.

4. Sprinkle the flaked almonds over the almond cream. Dust the tops with icing sugar. Bake for 15-20 minutes in the oven, still at the same temperature, until the almond cream is almost firm to the touch and golden brown on top.

5. Grind the basil, lemon zest and granulated sugar together in a mortar and pestle. Sprinkle the basil sugar over the top of the gratin.

6. You can serve the gratin hot, warm, or at room temperature with the crème fraîche.

CRÈME PÂTISSIÈRE

I live in England and my sons were born here so I'll always love this country, but I'm a Francophile too, so to call this 'thick custard' just doesn't give me the kick I get from 'la crème pâtissière' ('pastry cream'). So it's fitting that I learnt to make this crème from a Frenchman, the brilliant Benoît Blin, king of pastry at Le Manoir aux Quat'Saisons.

Traditionally the crème ('crème pat' for short) is a filling for tarts topped with fruits, but it can become anything from a soufflé to a crêpe stuffing. Adding the sugar to the milk before you heat it means that the milk doesn't burn onto the bottom of the pan.

Makes Approx. 1.3kg

Storage Fridge 4 days.
   Freezer 3 months

Prep/cooking time 25 mins

Active time 25 mins

. . . .

1 litre full-cream organic milk

200g caster sugar

1 vanilla pod

12 large egg yolks

50g plain flour

40g cornflour

1. Start by getting the very clean, plastic containers that you are going to store the crème in ready. It is best to fill them while the crème is still hot.

2. Get a large (24cm) thick-bottomed stainless-steel saucepan. Add the milk and sugar. Use a small, sharp knife to split the vanilla pod in half. Scrape out the seeds and add them with the empty pod to the saucepan. Put the pan on a medium to high heat. Bring the milk to simmering point, but don't boil it. Work next to your cooker while the milk heats as it can boil over very quickly.

3. Get a large bowl, add the egg yolks and the plain flour. Whisk together thoroughly. Add the cornflour. Whisk together thoroughly.

4. Once the milk has come to the simmer, pour it very slowly over the egg yolk mixture in the bowl, whisking continuously until everything is well combined and there are no lumps.

5. Pour the mixture back into the saucepan. Put the pan on a low to medium heat. Gently bring to the boil, whisking continuously. Make sure that you reach into the bottom corners and edges of the pan so that you don't get any lumps. The crème thickens a lot so will not come to a rolling boil, but it will bubble and spit like a volcano. Once the crème does this, cook and stir for a further minute so that the flour thickens the crème and you cook out the flour's taste.

6. Take the pan off the heat.

How to store

I freeze the crème in weights that are the multiples of the recipes I will use it for (100g for 4 portions of soufflé, 400g for 4 portions of brûlée, etc.).

Use a spatula to spread the crème into your containers. Cover with clingfilm, pushing it down to directly touch the surface of the crème to stop a skin forming on top. Leave to cool then seal the containers with a clean, preferably airtight lid. Refrigerate and/or freeze. When you defrost crème pâtissière, it tends to look as if it has separated. Don't worry, just whisk it thoroughly and it is as good as new again.

CRÈME PÂTISSIÈRE
MAGIC IDEAS

Once you have crème pâtissière in your Magic Fridge or Freezer it can be burnt, baked, flavoured, folded and spread. The crème brûlée ideas came from the recipe I developed with pear and ginger (p.204) specifically for this book: the texture is just like a baked custard. I know how popular crème brûlée is, so we'll concentrate on simple variations on them here. Choose your flavours, add some sugar, grab a blowtorch and you'll be amazed at the magic we can make.

FLAVOURED CRÈME PÂTISSIÈRES Transform your crème to one of these variations, by adding enough of the flavour you fancy to suit your taste: Grated ginger • Grated lemon, lime, orange or grapefruit zest • Reduced lemon, lime, orange or grapefruit juice (reduce the juice by ³/₄ to get a very concentrated citrus flavour) • Grand Marnier or Cointreau • Rum and raisins • Sherry and currants • Malibu and desiccated coconut • Marmalade • Raspberry or blackberry jam (p.220), apricot or blackcurrant jam • Orange-flower water • Passionfruit • Sliced basil or mint.

LIGHTER CRÈME PÂTISSIÈRES You can add anything from the list below to your basic crème pâtissière. It is roughly 2 parts crème to 1 part cream or yoghurt. Go by taste with the jam or curd: Ricotta cheese • Quark • Double cream • Whipped cream • Crème fraîche • Greek yoghurt • Raspberry or passionfruit yoghurt • Jam (p.220) • Lemon curd (p.208). These can also be made into crème brûlées or served with fruit, on pastry, scones, toast and croissants and in pancakes.

CRÈME PÂTISSIÈRE BRÛLÉES To make a good crème brûlée you need to start off with the right equipment. A blowtorch is vital to caramelise the sugar on top as it's hard to find a domestic grill that's hot enough. Buy some shallow dishes (like the ones on p.205) too. They're by far and away the best dishes for brûlées because they give you a large surface to caramelise so you get a better balance of crunch and crème: in a ramekin or cup you generally run out of the caramel before you've finished the custard.

The basic mixture is 200g crème pâtissière to 100g mascarpone cheese. You need to warm the crème pâtissière slightly in your microwave or in a saucepan. Whisk it until there are no lumps, then whisk in the mascarpone. This gives you roughly the texture of a baked custard and is best served around kitchen temperature. Fill your dishes with the mixture, then sprinkle caster sugar evenly over the top. Caramelise with a blowtorch as described on p.204.

FRUITY BRÛLÉES

Make one of the fruit mixtures below, then spread it over the base of your dishes. Spread the crème pâtissiére brûlée mixture over the top. Cover the top with caster sugar and caramelise with a blowtorch. The crème pâtissière mixture is a huge advantage for these, as you can put fruit underneath or in the crème without making the texture grainy and watery as you would if you added fruit into a baked custard before you cooked it.

Berry: Mix berries with berry purée or bottled smoothie. Season with caster sugar and lemon.

Apricot: Chop dried and tinned (or very ripe fresh) apricots together. Add vanilla seeds or good-quality extract. Purée a quarter of the apricots with a little syrup from the tin. Mix the purée and chopped apricots together. Season with caster sugar and lemon.

Banana: Slice bananas, toss with lime and, if you want a real treat, dulce de leche.

MULTI-LAYERED CRÈME BRÛLÉES

Smooth a layer of lemon curd (p.208) or chocolate mousse (p.232) halfway up a shallow dish. Fill it to the top with crème pâtissière brûlée mixture. Sprinkle sugar over the top and caramelise with a blowtorch.

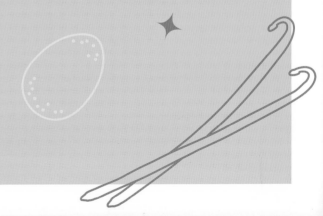

Berries & crème with glazed filo pastry

Crème pâtissière mixed with cream becomes 'crème diplomat' or 'crème légère' (light cream). This dessert is a layered arrangement that the French call 'mille feuille' (a thousand leaves), which I've always found pretty to say, let alone to look at. The crisp pastry and the sharp and sweet berries are held together by the crème for balance, taste and structure. A clever trick to bring out the flavour of any berries is to season them with a touch of caster sugar and lemon, then let them sit for 5 minutes before using.

Serves 2

Prep/cooking time 30 mins

Active time 30 mins

. . . .

1 sheet filo pastry, halved lengthways

25g unsalted butter, melted

30g icing sugar

★ 200g crème pâtissière (p.196)

150ml double cream

250g berries (a single type of berry or a mixture; I go by whatever's ripest)

1 tbsp caster sugar, or more to taste

1 tbsp lemon juice, or more to taste

1. Preheat your oven to 190°C/Gas 5, rack position upper middle shelf. Put a cooling rack next to your cooker.

2. Start with the filo pastry. Line a baking sheet with a re-usable non-stick mat. Lay half a filo sheet flat on your chopping board. Brush it with half the melted butter. Dust the filo lightly with icing sugar. Top the filo with the second half filo sheet. Press down well. Brush with the remainder of the butter.

3. Cut the pastry into 6 x 12-15cm irregular triangles. (Use a ruler, it'll make your life much easier.) Lay these 6 triangles in a single layer on the lined baking sheet. Dust the filo very heavily but evenly with the rest of the icing sugar. Bake for 5-7 minutes in the preheated oven until glazed and golden. (If your oven has a hot spot at the back you'll need to turn the baking sheet halfway through and it may be that you need to take some of the pastry triangles that are ready off the tray before the others.) Once the pastry is baked, use a wide palette knife to transfer it to the cooling rack while it is still warm or the triangles will stick and break when you try to get them off the tray.

4. While the pastry cooks and cools, make the crème diplomat. Get a large bowl. Add the crème pâtissière. Whisk the crème until it has the texture of mayonnaise. In a separate bowl, whip the double cream to soft peaks. Fold the two together, you don't have to be too gentle with this.

5. Toss the berries with the caster sugar and lemon juice.

6. To serve, turn the pastry upside down, the underside is the most beautifully glazed. Put a blob of crème in the middle of your plates. Top 4 triangles of pastry with a spoonful of the crème. Spread it to the edges. Put a quarter of the berries on top of each. Put a blob of crème on top of each to help the pastry stick. Put 2 of the triangles on top of the other 2. Put the final empty pastry triangle on top.

7. Use a big fish slice to put each pastry stack onto your plates.

Dulce de leche soufflé with mango salad

The secret to successful soufflés is to take great care with every step of the recipe. Make sure that everything else is ready and that the oven is at the right temperature before you start to whip the egg whites. The egg whites must be good and firm before you add the sugar, which you add slowly and keep whipping until you have very stiff peaks. And, of course, make sure that you begin with the Magic crème pâtissière.

If you fancy a boozy soufflé, add a tablespoon of Cognac, rum or Grand Marnier to the crème pâtissière.

Serves 2
Prep/cooking time 35 mins
Active time 20-25 mins

. . . .

100g mango flesh (½ small mango), cut into 1cm dice

1 passionfruit

Grated zest of ½ lime and 2 tsp juice

60g caster sugar, plus extra to season the mango and to line the moulds

20g soft unsalted butter

★ 50g crème pâtissière (p.196)

30g dulce de leche

2 large egg whites

Icing sugar, for dusting

1. Preheat your oven to 180°C/Gas 4, rack position middle shelf.

2. Start with the mango salad. Get a small bowl. Add the diced mango flesh. Cut the passionfruit in half. Scoop the seeds onto the mango. Grate the lime zest over the top. Stir it all together. Season with the lime juice and sugar to taste.

3. Get 2 x 175-200ml ramekin dishes. Brush their insides with the soft butter, making sure that there are no gaps. Sprinkle caster sugar all over the butter. Shake off any excess sugar.

4. Get a large bowl. Add the crème pâtissière. Warm it slightly (your microwave is best for this). Whisk the crème until it is smooth. Add the dulce de leche, and whisk the two together until the mixture is totally smooth.

5. For the best results, use an electric mixer. Add the egg whites and 1 tsp lime juice to the mixer bowl. Whisk the egg white to firm peaks. Add the 60g caster sugar 1 tsp at a time, whisking for 10 seconds between each addition. Once all the sugar is incorporated, whisk until the egg whites are firm and glossy.

6. Use a rubber spatula to stir a third of the egg whites into the crème and dulce mixture. Gently fold in the remaining egg whites. Once they are mixed, stop folding, so as not to knock air out.

7. Fill the soufflé dishes with the soufflé mixture. Smooth over the tops with a palette knife. Rub your thumb around the edge of the ramekin to push the soufflé mixture away from the edge. Put the soufflé dishes onto a baking sheet so that you can take them out of the oven easily.

8. Bake the soufflés for 10-12 minutes in your preheated oven. They need to be well risen and look dry around the sides as in the photo.

9. While they bake, put the mango salad and icing sugar on your table with your cutlery so that all you have to do is carry the soufflés to the table once they are ready. Dust the tops with icing sugar.

Pear, ginger & lime crème pâtissière brûlée

I first came across the glorious combination of pear, ginger, lime and cream in the brilliant book that brought me to Europe - Raymond Blanc's Recipes from Le Manoir aux Quat'Saisons. He makes a magical puff pastry and lime crème anglaise confection topped with pears simmered in ginger butterscotch. I've just looked at the photo and my mouth waters as it did when I first saw it over 25 years ago and again when, a few years later, I travelled halfway around the world to taste the real thing.

This recipe shows you how to make a crème brûlée from crème pâtissière, a great little trick (and there are more examples on the Magic Ideas pages). Shallow dishes, 12.5cm wide and 3cm deep are ideal to prepare these brûlées in; if you don't have any, and need to use cups or ramekins, cut the pear into dice to mix with the crème.

Serves 2
Prep/cooking time 15 mins
Active time 15 mins

. . . .

★ 200g crème pâtissière
(p.196)

100g mascarpone cheese

10g peeled and grated
fresh root ginger

Grated zest of 1 lime

3 tinned pear halves

4 tbsp caster sugar

1. Start with the crème mixture. Get a medium-sized bowl. Add the crème pâtissière. Warm it through slightly (this works best in the microwave) then whisk until there are no lumps. Whisk in the mascarpone, followed by the ginger and the lime zest.

2. Next, prepare the pears. Pat them as dry as you possibly can with kitchen paper. Cut the rounded bottom off two of the halves so that they will sit flat in your dishes. Cut the trimmings and the third pear half into small (1cm) dice.

3. Stir the diced pear into the crème pâtissière mix. Spread it into your dishes. Push the pear halves into the middle so that they lie flat and at the same level as the crème. Smooth a little of the crème into the hole where the pear's core would have been.

4. Sprinkle 2 tbsp caster sugar very evenly over the top of each crème. Wipe the sides of the dishes after you do, or the sugar will burn onto the rims and make the serving dishes hard to wash up.

5. Caramelise the sugar with a blowtorch. Start from about 10cm away to first melt the sugar then move closer to caramelise it.

Upside-down apricot crème, basil & almond tart

Almonds, apricots and crème pâtissière are great old friends. Basil is the newcomer here. I first discovered that basil loves apricots when I was making jam and pistou at the same time in Provence. I licked my fingers at just the right moment for the two to become imprinted on my memory.

It's hard to make the base for the almond 'pastry' that goes on top in smaller quantities, so just put what's left over in your Magic Fridge, where it will keep for months. If you fancy a quickie, the tart can be tasty without the 'pastry'. You could crumble some gingernut biscuits or scatter some toasted almonds over the top.

Serves 2
Prep/cooking time 25 mins
Active time 25 mins

. . . .

40g unsalted butter

40g caster sugar

2 tbsp honey or, ideally, liquid glucose

60g flaked almonds

★ 150g crème pâtissière (p.196)

100g apricot jam

2 tbsp syrup from the apricot tin

10 tinned apricot halves in syrup

3 tbsp sliced basil

2 tbsp crème fraîche

1. Preheat your oven to 180°C/Gas 4, rack position middle shelf. Boil your kettle. Put a cooling rack beside your cooker.

2. Get a small (16-18cm) saucepan. Add the butter, sugar and honey. Slowly bring to the boil over a medium heat. Once the sugar is completely dissolved take the pan off the heat. Stir in the flaked almonds. Make sure that everything is thoroughly combined. Weigh 3 (always make at least 1 extra) 25g spoonfuls.

3. Line a baking sheet with a re-usable non-stick mat. Put the 3 spoonfuls of almond mixture on top with plenty of space between them.

4. Flatten the piles of almond mixture with the back of a spoon dipped in boiling water, just a little, as they will spread a lot further as they cook. Bake in your preheated oven for 6-7 minutes or until they are golden, there should be no white at all. They become irregular shapes, which is completely normal. (There was a little hole in the one I used for the photo that you can some crème poking through!) You may need to turn the baking sheet halfway through. Take the baking sheet out of your oven. Leave the 'pastries' for about 2 minutes until they harden enough for you to gently transfer them from the non-stick mat to the cooling rack.

5. Next get a small bowl. Add the crème pâtissière. If it is straight from the fridge, warm it slightly (your microwave is best) and whisk it smooth. Add 50g of the apricot jam. Whisk together.

6. Get a shallow bowl or dish and add the rest of the apricot jam and the 2 tbsp syrup from the tin. Whisk together. Add the apricot halves, and toss to coat them with the syrup. Stir in the basil.

7. Spoon the apricots and syrup onto your plates. Put the apricot crème pâtissière into the middle. Spoon the apricots and syrup over the top. Add the crème fraîche. Put the almond 'pastry' on top.

LEMON CURD

In the south of France, the lemon is said to represent the sun here on earth. A glorious idea that I've brought to the Magic Fridge, where the lemon curd provides sunshine and joy at any time of day. If possible, get the best, unsprayed lemons you can for this; the zest is a huge part of the flavour and the better your lemons the more intense the zest's flavour will be. Lemon curd seems to keep forever, but in my experience it's an impossible temptation so forever is never more than a couple of weeks.

Makes Slightly less than 1kg

Storage Unopened, fridge 1 month. Opened, fridge 2-3 days. Freezer 3 months

Prep/cooking time 20 mins

Active time 20 mins

. . . .

4 large eggs

4 large egg yolks

200g caster sugar

Grated zest of 4 unsprayed lemons and 200ml juice

200g unsalted butter, cut into small dice

1. Get a large (24cm), thick-bottomed stainless-steel saucepan. Add the eggs, egg yolks, sugar, lemon zest and lemon juice. Whisk together until all of the ingredients are well combined. Add the butter.

2. Whisk over a medium heat until the mixture thickens to the texture of thick custard. Make sure you get the whisk right into the corners so that the lemon curd doesn't curdle. When you make lemon curd for the first time, please feel free to cook it over a lower temperature. It'll take a bit longer but it's safer and you don't get any surprises like the curd boiling and scrambling at the corners. If you have a thermometer, 80°C is a good temperature to get to. At this stage you can put the lemon curd into a blender and blend for a minute or so to make it lighter in texture and colour - it goes almost mousse like.

How to store

Store in clean, preferably sterilised jars, of the size that you are most likely to use up in one go. Fill the jars right up to the top. Put a piece of clingfilm directly on the surface to stop a skin forming. Put the lids on the jars. Leave to cool. Store in the fridge (or freeze in freezer-proof containers).

Once the lemon curd is open, it can keep for 2-3 days, or even longer, but be very careful to make sure the sides of the jar are clean and you keep a piece of clingfilm directly touching the surface. The most important thing is to keep the air away from the food. Use a clean spoon and don't put your fingers into the curd unless you are going to finish the whole jar.

LEMON CURD
MAGIC IDEAS

Lemon curd can be a spread for your breakfast toast, a dip for a mid-morning fruity snack, a marvellous marbling for a lunchtime yoghurt, a bonus on your biscuit at afternoon tea and a crème brûlée after dinner. Because it is so light and has the lemon's bite, it's a pick-me-up for anytime. You can spread lemon curd on madeleines, muffins, biscuits and bananas for a super refreshing afternoon tea, use lemon curd as a dip for orange or grapefruit segments. For very speedy snacks you can serve lemon curd with granola, as a dip for fresh strawberries, stirred into a tin of rice pudding, with ice cream, or you can simply eat the curd out of the jar and enjoy a moment of citrus-scented bliss.

FLAVOURED LEMON CURD Mix your lemon curd with any of the following: Orange and grapefruit zest • Passionfruit pulp • Dulce de leche • Freshly grated ginger • Vanilla seeds.

FRUITY AND FROZEN LEMON YOGHURT To make a delicious breakfast treat, fold together yoghurt, lemon curd and blackberry or blackcurrant jam, just enough to marble the mixture. Sprinkle oats over the top for a bit of extra guts to get you through to lunchtime. For a multi-layered citrus spectacular, whisk lemon marmalade into yoghurt then streak it with lemon curd; this freezes well to make frozen yoghurt too.

FRUITY PORRIDGE On a cold day, start the other way around. Use the oats to make porridge then stir in the curd and jam.

COLD FRUIT SALAD WITH LEMON CURD Make a cold salad of fresh peaches or berries in summer, figs or plums in autumn, or pears, pineapple or banana in winter, all to serve with a dollop of lemon curd.

HOT FRUIT SALAD WITH LEMON CURD Roast peaches, pears, pineapple or figs with butter or olive oil and honey in an oven at 200°C/Gas 6 (the time will depend on the ripeness of the specific fruits). Serve with a dollop of lemon curd.

LEMON CRÈME BRÛLÉE Mix 2 parts lemon curd together with 1 part mascarpone cheese. Spread into shallow dishes, sprinkle caster sugar evenly over the top, then use a blowtorch to caramelise the top.

MARBLED LEMON CURD MOUSSE Fold 2 parts lemon curd together with 1 part whipped double cream. Just barely mix in 1 more part of lemon curd so that it streaks the mousse. This is delicious with raspberries and basil sugar (p.228).

CITRUS SALAD WITH LEMON CURD Peel a mixture of citrus fruit, including blood oranges if you can get them. Slice the fruit and spread it over flat plates. Sprinkle with citrus sugar (p.259), then serve with a dollop of lemon curd.

BERRY SALAD WITH LEMON CURD Streak lemon curd with strawberry jam then serve with fresh strawberries, or use raspberry jam (p.220) and serve with fresh raspberries.

LEMON CURD ETON MESS Mix lemon curd with citrus segments or berries, broken-up meringues from the shop and whipped cream. I like ice cream or sorbet with this too.

Banana, lemon curd & passionfruit hedgehog

This is a wonderful riff on an old-fashioned banana split. The hedgehog spikes are quicker to attach than you may think and enormous fun to make. I get a couple of sticky-fingered little helpers to help with mine, but if you want to go rustic, just scatter the almonds over the top. You need to pick out curvy bananas to get the body shape required for your hedgehogs.

Serves 2
Prep/cooking time 20 mins
Active time 20 mins

. . . .

75ml double cream

★ 100g lemon curd (p.208), plus 2 tbsp

2 passionfruit, cut in half

1 tbsp water

1 tbsp caster sugar

Zest of ½ lime, removed with a zester, and 2 tbsp juice

2 medium-sized curvy bananas

2 scoops vanilla, lemon or passionfruit ice cream, or frozen yoghurt

3–4 tbsp flaked almonds

1. Fill and boil your kettle to have hot water ready for your scoop and spoon.

2. Start with the marbled cream. Get a medium-sized bowl. Add the double cream. Whip the cream to soft peaks. Use a spatula to add the 100g lemon curd, then mix the two together barely enough to make streaks through the cream.

3. Get a small bowl. Add the passionfruit pulp, water, sugar and lime zest. Stir together.

4. Peel the bananas. Cut them in half lengthways on an angle. Put them on the plates you are going to serve them on. Join the halves together with the rounded side facing outwards to make 2 oval shapes. Brush each banana with 1 tbsp of lime juice.

5. Put 1 tbsp of lemon curd in the middle of each banana oval. Put a ball of ice cream on top.

6. Spoon the marbled lemon curd cream over the ice cream. Dip a tablespoon into boiling water then smooth this lemon curd cream into an oval dome.

7. Stud each dome with flaked almonds to create the hedgehog effect. Spoon the passionfruit mixture over everything. Serve.

James' lemon curd
& strawberry 'Mont Blanc'

My son James came up with this dessert when I was in the middle of an adventure with chestnut purée. I made my version of the traditional Mont Blanc and while we were eating it James suggested doing something similar with lemon curd and strawberries. He perfected it when my Uncle John came from New Zealand to stay, and it's a fantastic fairy tale of a pudding: 'Awesome', as James would say. Serving desserts in glasses is a practical way to give things structure without having to encase them in cake or pastry. I've often got some homemade meringue in my Magic Freezer, but the little ones that you can buy are fine for this.

The combination of curd, ice cream and meringue is incredibly greedy and I unapologetically love it. As long as you've got these three, the options are endless.

Serves 2
Prep/cooking time 30 mins
Active time 30 mins

· ·

160g strawberries

80g strawberry jam

★ 160g lemon curd (p.208)

4 little meringues

2 balls vanilla (or strawberry or lemon) ice cream

Icing sugar, for dusting

1. Get some shiny glasses or small glass bowls ready.

2. Start with the strawberries. Pull or cut out their green tops. Cut each strawberry into quarters.

3. Get a small shallow bowl. Add the strawberries and jam. Gently mix them together until the strawberries are lightly glazed with the jam. Spoon a sixth of the glazed strawberries into each glass.

4. If you have a piping bag, use it for the lemon curd. This makes life much easier. Pipe or spoon a quarter of the lemon curd over the top of the strawberries in each glass.

5. Crush 1 meringue into the middle of the curd in each glass.

6. Spoon a sixth of the glazed strawberries into each glass.

7. Spoon or pipe the remaining lemon curd over the strawberries.

8. Spoon the rest of the glazed strawberries over the top. If you are making the desserts in advance, prepare them up to here.

9. To serve, scoop a ball of ice cream on top of the last layer of strawberries. Put a meringue on top of each. Dust with icing sugar.

Jake's lemon curd
& blackcurrant jam French toast

This combination was my eldest son Jake's idea for Mother's Day one year. I'd never seen French toast with a stuffing before and I love food that oozes from the inside, so it has become a plaything of mine. I've tried many variations but Jake's combination of lemon curd and blackcurrant is the most dramatic and delicious.

Using the lemon curd as a base you could try all sorts of raw and cooked fruit combinations to introduce new tastes for kids.

Serves 2

Prep/cooking time
15-20 mins

Active time 15-20 mins

. . . .

75ml double cream,
  plus 90ml

 60g lemon curd (p.208),
  plus 100g

50g blackcurrant jam,
  plus 40g

75ml full-cream milk

2 heaped tbsp caster sugar,
  plus 1 heaped tbsp

Grated zest of 1 lemon

4 x 2cm-thick brioche slices

2 large eggs

50g unsalted butter

1. Start with the whipped cream mixture. Get a medium-sized bowl. Lightly whip the 75ml cream. Add the 60g lemon curd and the 50g blackcurrant jam. Stir once or twice, barely enough to marble the cream. Store the marbled cream in your fridge.

2. Next get a medium-sized (20cm) shallow pan. Add the milk, 90ml cream, 2 tbsp caster sugar and the lemon zest. Mix together. Bring to the boil then take the pan off the heat. Soak the brioche slices in this mixture for 1 minute on each side while the milk mixture is still warm.

3. Beat the eggs and 1 heaped tbsp caster sugar together in a shallow dish. Soak the brioche for 45 seconds each side in this mixture.

4. Spread the 100g lemon curd not quite to the edges of 2 soaked brioche slices. Put half the remaining jam into the middle of each. Put a second soaked brioche slice on top of each.

5. Heat a large non-stick frying pan with the butter until it is golden.

6. Fry the French toasts for 90 seconds on each side over a very stable medium heat. Turn it to low if you need to: the butter should not burn, but it needs to be hot enough to crisp and brown the outside. Serve the filled French toasts with the marbled cream.

Upside-down lemon meringue pie

If there is lemon curd, there must be lemon meringue pie. This is my magic one: make it in glasses, bowls or jars and make sure you get a little of each layer when you eat it. The technique I've used for the pastry turns filo into sweet citrus pastry. The middle layer of butter, sugar and zest is vital to stick the sheets of pastry together, and to flavour the pastry all the way to the burnished glaze on top.

This is a great dessert for kids to assemble. They can reflect their personalities in the layers they make and discover that uniform or higgledy piggledy will both taste good.

Serves 2

Prep/cooking time 20 mins

Active time 20 mins

. . . .

25g unsalted butter

1 red grapefruit

30g icing sugar

1 sheet filo pastry

150g crème fraîche

★ 200g lemon curd (p.208)

15g meringue (1 normal-sized nest, or 5 small ones)

1. Preheat your oven to 180°C/Gas 4, rack position upper middle shelf. Put a cooling rack next to your cooker. Line a baking sheet with a re-usable non-stick mat.

2. Start with the butter. Put it into a small bowl. Finely grate half of the grapefruit zest into the butter. Melt the butter in your microwave (or in a small pan on your cooker). Sieve in the icing sugar. Stir until the mixture is completely smooth.

3. Lay the filo sheet flat on your work surface. Cut it in half lengthways. Brush half of it with half of the melted grapefruit butter. Put the second half on top. Press down thoroughly. Brush the top with the rest of the grapefruit butter. (If the butter becomes hard to spread, warm it slightly and don't worry if it becomes a little clumpy, it'll be fine once it's baked.) Cut out 2 circles around the top opening of the bowls you are going to serve the pie in. Put the pastry circles upside down onto your lined baking sheet. Bake the trimmings for snacks as well.

4. Bake the pastry for 5–6 minutes in the preheated oven until it is glazed and golden. Set a timer, as these burn very quickly. (If your oven has a hot spot at the back you'll need to turn them halfway through.) Use a palette knife to transfer the pastry to the cooling rack while it is still hot so that it doesn't stick.

5. Cut the top and bottom off the grapefruit so that it sits flat on your chopping board. Cut away the peel in strips, being sure to get rid of all of the white pith. Hold the grapefruit over a small bowl then cut out each segment of flesh between the white membranes. Once you have cut out all of the segments, squeeze the juice from the membranes into the bowl. Cut each segment in half.

6. Put the grapefruit segments and juice into the bottom of your bowls or glasses. Spoon the crème fraîche over the top. Spoon half the lemon curd over the crème fraîche. Break the meringue into chunks over the lemon curd. Spread the rest of the lemon curd over the meringue. Put the pastry on top.

RASPBERRY (OR BLACKBERRY) JAM

The wonderful custom of preserving fruit when it's at the height of its beauty and bounty is the most familiar illustration of the idea behind *The Magic Fridge*. As good as jam is on toast, it has many more uses: jam comforts you, mixed with fresh fruit it enhances, and with any sort of cream or ice cream it explodes into life. The trick to making this jam beautifully is firstly to use raspberries or blackberries that are as ripe as possible but with no mould; to use jam sugar (sugar with added pectin), so that you can cook the jam quickly to keep the fresh berry flavour but still have jam that sets; not to stir too much; and to let the jam almost set before bottling so that the fruit is well distributed.

This amount is the maximum that I would suggest making at one time unless you have a special large and low-sided preserving pan.

Any time you can, introduce your kids to the magic of making jam and, if you can, take them to pick wild blackberries to make it with.

Makes Slightly less than 1.9kg
Storage Fridge 3 months
Prep/cooking time 20 mins
Active time 20 mins

. . . .

1kg jam sugar
Grated zest of 1 orange
Grated zest and juice (3 tbsp) of 1 lemon
1kg raspberries or blackberries

1. Get a large (24cm) heavy-bottomed saucepan. Add the jam sugar, the citrus zest and the lemon juice. Add the raspberries. Give it all a gentle toss rather than stir so as not to break up the raspberries.

2. Gently bring the raspberry mixture to the boil. Watch over it lovingly, to make sure that the sugar dissolves before it starts to boil. Stir occasionally to make sure that the jam doesn't stick to the bottom.

3. Once the jam boils, boil rapidly for 4-5 minutes, stirring every now and then. The temperature should be 104°C. Take the pan off the heat.

4. Pour the jam into a bowl. Stir gently every now and then as it cools. This will help distribute the fruit evenly.

How to store

Spoon the fruit into small, clean, preferably sterilised jars just before the jam has set. Fill the jars right up to the top. Cover the jars first with clingfilm, which should touch the surface of the jam, then with the lids. Leave to cool. Store in the fridge or a cool place.

RASPBERRY (OR BLACKBERRY) JAM
MAGIC IDEAS

Jam has become such an everyday food that it's easy to forget that this sticky mixture of fruit and sugar is a treat. It can be served with, on, or as the base for a great many different desserts and it can be a sauce, a seasoning or a dip. Raspberry and blackberry have enough acidity to bring bite as well as sweetness to everything they touch.

RASPBERRY AND PINE NUT JAM Add untoasted pine nuts to the jam as it sets and they will suspend throughout the jam like jewels. It's a startling combination in taste and texture, the fat and flavoursome berries are offset perfectly by the creamy pine nuts.

JAM AS SWEET SEASONING Think of jam as a sweet salad dressing. Liquefying jam by gently warming it to mix with fresh berries has a fire-cracking effect on both. I like to use the same jam and fruit together for a singular intensity, but it's also lovely with one jam and a mixture of berries. You use just enough jam to coat the berries so that you don't make them too sweet. The jam enhances and concentrates the flavour of the fruit and the fruit does the same for the jam. It's the ultimate seasoning, as you are taking your ingredients and making them taste more intensely of themselves.

WARM BERRY SOUP Here you add enough juice or water to the jam to give it a texture that lightly coats the back of a spoon then bring it to the boil. Add berries, barely warm them through, spoon it all into bowls and serve with vanilla ice cream or berry sorbet. Eat this quite quickly and without talking so that the ice cream or sorbet doesn't melt completely. It's so delicious that this won't be a problem at all.

JAM WITH CHEESE Blackberry jam is slightly better suited to this than raspberry, but either can be spread thinly on toast or cracker then topped with creamy goat's cheese or soft blue cheese.

UPSIDE-DOWN CHEESECAKE IN A GLASS Crush up ginger biscuits and bind them with a touch of olive oil. Spoon jam into the bottom of a glass. Mix cream cheese with lemon juice and icing sugar to taste. Marble the cream cheese with a little jam. Spoon it on top of the jam, then finish with the crushed biscuits.

RASPBERRY JAM AND YOGHURT BRÛLÉE Whisk together 2 parts very thick Greek yoghurt with 1 part raspberry jam until the mixture is smooth and pink. Add the same amount of jam again and stir it just once or twice, enough to marble the dark jam through the pink yoghurt. Spread the mixture into shallow dishes. Freeze for an hour or so to harden the mixture. Sprinkle caster sugar over the top. Caramelise with a blowtorch.

HOT AND COLD RASPBERRY-RIPPLE ICE CREAM Heat raspberry jam and spoon it over scoops of vanilla ice cream. The jam will ripple the ice cream and create an instant sauce that is a mixture of the two.

UPSIDE-DOWN TARTS Bake one of the 'pastry' tops on p.206. Mix raspberries or blackberries with jam and put them onto a plate. Spoon whipped cream with vanilla (p.234) or crème pâtissière (p.196) into the middle and then top with the 'pastry'.

JAM AND PANCAKES Spread warmed pancakes (p.172) with jam and top them with fresh berries for breakfast. Add ice cream or cream to make it a dessert.

JAM AND SPONGE CAKE Whenever you make a tiered sponge cake (p.254), it will be made much more special if you spread it with jam before your layers of cream.

JAM AND LEMON CURD The combination of these two (see p.208 for lemon curd) is one of my favourite things to serve alongside anything from fruit to cake to pancakes to croissants.

Autumn pudding

English autumn fruit inspires this pudding; along with Provençal figs, wild English blackberries and damson plums are the tastiest of all fruit to cook. My autumn pudding can be served cold, but is at its best warm. As it's a greedy Mackay pud, I serve it with both crème fraîche and ice cream, but you could have either, neither, or a jug of pouring cream.

Serves 2

Prep/cooking time 30 mins

Active time 30 mins

. . . .

5 medium-thick slices white bread, crusts cut off

1 tsp vegetable oil

9 tbsp raspberry or blackberry jam (p.220)

6 tbsp water

150g damsons, dark plums or a mixture, de-stoned, chopped into 2cm pieces

2 tbsp caster sugar

125g (or close, 1 small punnet) blackberries (frozen are fine, so is a frozen berry mixture)

2 balls vanilla ice cream

4 tbsp crème fraîche

1. Start with the bread and jam. Cut 2 x 7cm circles to fit your ramekins' bases from 1 side of 2 of the bread slices. Cut a rectangle large enough to come up the sides of the ramekins from the other side of each slice. You should have 2 circles, and 2 rectangles. Cut another 1 slice of bread in half lengthways. Cut 2 x 8cm circles from the final 2 bread slices. You should finish with 4 rectangles, 2 x 8cm circles and 2 x 7cm circles.

2. Lightly brush your ramekins with oil. Line them with a double layer of clingfilm, leaving plenty of overlap at the sides.

3. Get a small (16-18cm) saucepan. Add 6 tbsp jam and 4 tbsp water. Warm over a medium heat, stirring constantly, until the jam has melted to the point that it barely coats the back of a spoon. Take the pan off the heat.

4. Dip the smaller bread circles in the hot jam; turn them over to fully soak them. Put the soaked slices into the bottom of the lined ramekins. Brush the 4 rectangles on 1 side only with the jam. Put these around the outside of the ramekins with the jammy side facing out. Brush the large circles on both sides with the jam and set aside. Keep the pan and any jam left in it to cook the fruit in.

5. Add the chopped plums, 2 tbsp water, sugar and 3 tbsp jam to the pan. Put the lid on. Simmer gently for 7-10 minutes or until the plums are soft. Take the lid off. Add the blackberries (or mixed berries). Simmer for 1 minute. Take the pan off the heat.

6. Spoon as much fruit and juice as you need into the lined ramekins for it to come just to the top. Put the large bread circles on top. Pull the overlapping clingfilm over the top of the bread in each ramekin, it will be slightly mounded. Seal tightly. Put the ramekins onto a plate. Put a second plate on top. Weigh this down with 1.2kg (3 full tins of beans).

7. To serve, warm (rather than heat, if they are too hot, they may collapse) the puddings for 1 minute in your microwave. Open the clingfilm. Turn the puddings out onto plates. Warm the remaining juice and any leftover fruit to spoon over the top. Serve with ice cream and crème fraîche.

Hot summer fruit & jam pie

I once read the phrase 'as warm as a jaguar's breath' to describe Alain Ducasse's warm wild strawberry soup. The writer must have had a close shave with a wild cat to get that sentence but I reckon it was worth it. These pies come out of the oven steaming hot, more like I'd imagine the breath of an angry lion to be, but the inspiration comes from the same 'fraises de bois au jus de fraises tièdes' in Monaco. I'd rarely used frozen berries until I started looking hard at ingredients for the Magic Freezer, but they are excellent to cook, generally good quality and cheaper than fresh. For a super-quick version, you can leave out the pastry: heat the berries with the jam in your microwave and eat them with cream or ice cream on top.

Serves 2

Prep/cooking time 30 mins

Active time 20 mins

. . . .

250g frozen mixed berries

★ 140g raspberry or blackberry jam (p.220)

1 large egg yolk

1 tbsp milk

1 sheet ready-rolled puff pastry, kept flat in the fridge until needed

100ml double cream

½ vanilla pod, split and scraped

20g icing sugar

2 scoops vanilla ice cream (optional)

1. Preheat your oven to 200°C/Gas 6, rack position middle shelf.

2. Get 2 single-portion-sized ovenproof dishes (or cups and saucers are quite fun for this) large enough to hold the berries comfortably. Put half of the berries into each. Spoon 70g of jam over each portion of berries.

3. Get a small bowl. Add the egg yolk and milk. Mix them together to make an eggwash.

4. Cut 2 circles from the pastry, each 6cm larger than the top of your dishes. They need to be this much larger so that there is plenty to stick them to the side of the dishes. Brush 1 side of each pastry circle with half the eggwash.

5. Next, you need to attach the pastry to the top of your dishes. Be careful with this, because if you stretch the pastry then it will cave in as it bakes. With the egg-washed sides facing downwards, cover the dishes with the pastry circles. Press gently around the sides to make sure that the overlapping pastry is well stuck on.

6. Brush the top with the rest of the eggwash.

7. Bake for 15 minutes in your preheated oven until the pastry is golden.

8. While the pastry bakes, make the vanilla cream. Get a medium-sized bowl. Pour in the cream. Add the vanilla seeds and icing sugar. Whip to soft peaks. Serve with the pies and some ice cream if you fancy it.

Panna cotta with raspberry jam & basil sugar

The jam sets this panna cotta off beautifully. For me the secret of a set cream dessert is to introduce a little acidity, and there is no better way to do this than to add crème fraîche. Basil sugar makes a wonderful seasoning for the top, like aromatic jewellery.

Serves 4

Prep/cooking time 25 mins, plus 3-4 hours' setting time

Active time 25 mins

. . . .

4g gelatine leaves

★ 240g raspberry or blackberry jam (p.220)

375ml whipping cream

110g caster sugar

1 vanilla pod, split and scraped

85g crème fraîche

10 large basil leaves

30g granulated sugar

125g raspberries

1. Start with the gelatine. Fill a medium-sized bowl with cold water. Add the gelatine. Soak for 5 minutes or until it softens.

2. Put the jam into the bottoms of 4 glasses. Put the glasses in your fridge.

3. Get a small (16-18cm) saucepan. Add the cream, caster sugar, vanilla seeds and vanilla pod. Whisk everything together. Warm the mixture to just under simmering point. Do not let it boil. Take the pan off the heat.

4. Squeeze the gelatine dry. Add it to the cream mixture and stir until it is completely dissolved. Leave to cool for 5 minutes. Take out the vanilla pod.

5. Put the crème fraîche into a large measuring jug. Gently whisk in the warm cream a little at a time until the mixture is smooth. Leave to cool for 10 minutes.

6. Take the 4 glasses out of your fridge. Carefully pour the cream against the inside of the glasses (this stops the cream and jam from combining, meaning that you can get clear layers) over the top of the jam. Leave to set for 3 hours in the fridge.

7. To make the basil sugar, put the basil and granulated sugar into a small mortar and pestle. Grind together until you have a coarse green powder.

8. Put the raspberries on top of the panna cottas. Sprinkle the basil sugar over the top.

Raspberry jam ripple frozen yoghurt

This is a simple way of making 'ice cream'. It's tangy, refreshing and delicious, just the thing for a summer's afternoon or a reviving breakfast.

You don't absolutely need an ice cream machine for this recipe but the texture will be smoother and lighter if the frozen yoghurt is made in one. I would highly recommend getting an ice cream machine for your birthday - it's like having a bit of Willy Wonka's factory at home. You can eat the raspberry yoghurt unfrozen, or put it into shallow dishes, chill them nearly to the point of freezing, and then caramelise the top as you would a crème brûlée.

Serves 2

Prep/cooking time 10 mins, plus 5-6 hours' freezing

Active time 10 mins

. . . .

1 x 250g tub full-fat yoghurt (the more fat the better), or fromage blanc

★ 250g raspberry or blackberry jam (p.220)

1. Get a shallow plastic or earthenware container. Add the yoghurt. Whisk in two-thirds of the raspberry jam.

2. Put the tray in the freezer and freeze for 6 hours, vigorously stirring the mixture every 30 minutes. (I found it easiest to leave my whisk in the dish in the freezer.) After about 3 hours, when the yoghurt begins to harden, take it out of the freezer and fold in the rest of the raspberry jam, combining the two just enough to make streaks through the mixture. Freeze for a further 2-3 hours before serving.

3. If you have an ice cream machine, just pour the original mixture into it and churn. Once it is ready, add the final third of the raspberry jam and churn once or twice until it streaks through the mixture.

4. Serve on frozen plates or in frozen glasses.

CHOCOLATE MOUSSE

This smouldering brown beauty is a kiss on the lips for true chocolate lovers. For depth of flavour, I always use chocolate containing 70% cocoa solids. A great mousse wants to be light enough to melt on your tongue but not so light that you lose the chocolate's intensity.

As you will discover in the pages to come, chocolate mousse can be served cold, warm or hot.

I try passionately to get my kids used to the taste of real chocolate: most milk chocolate and 'chocolate' snack-bars lack chocolate, lack flavour and are overloaded with sugar. The eggs are raw, so it's no good for pregnant women or tiny kids.

Makes Approx. 1kg

Storage Fridge 7 days.
Freezer 3 months

Prep/cooking time 20 mins,
plus 1 hour's setting time

Active time 20 mins

. . . .

320g 70% chocolate

150g unsalted butter, diced

50g unsweetened cocoa
powder

100ml boiling water

6 large eggs

100g caster sugar

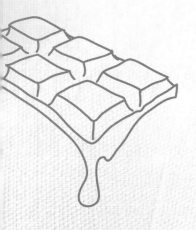

1. Get a saucepan that a medium-sized bowl will sit in comfortably without falling inside. Half-fill the pan with water. Put it on a medium heat to simmer. Break the chocolate into your bowl. Add the butter. Put the bowl over the pan of barely simmering hot water. Stir occasionally until the chocolate is fully melted. Once it is, take the pan off the heat but leave the bowl over the hot water.

2. Get a small (16-18cm) pan. Add the cocoa powder and the boiling water. Stir thoroughly until the cocoa is diluted. Stir the cocoa liquid into the melted chocolate and butter mixture.

3. Get a large shallow bowl and a small bowl. Separate the egg whites into the large bowl and the egg yolks into the small one. At this stage check the chocolate. It should be lukewarm when held to your lip: too hot and the mousse may separate; too cold and it will harden. (If you're not entirely sure, a little too hot is much safer than a little too cold.)

4. Whisk the egg whites to firm peaks with an electric mixer. Add the sugar 1 tbsp at a time, whisking well between each spoonful. Continue whisking until the egg whites are very firm and shiny. Gently fold in the egg yolks with a spatula.

5. Briskly stir one-third of the egg white and egg yolk mixture into the melted chocolate. Once it is completely combined, use a spatula to fold in the rest of the mixture gently but very quickly.

6. If you want to serve the mousse just as it is, this is enough for 10 portions. Use your spatula to transfer the chocolate mousse into dishes for the amount of people you want to serve now. Put them in your fridge to set for at least an hour.

How to store

I freeze or refrigerate any remaining mousse in weights that are multiples of the recipes I will use it for (180g for 2 portions of the boozy prunes, 200g for 4 portions of upside-down tart, etc.). Use very clean, plastic containers with tight-fitting lids. The key for long storage is cleanliness.

CHOCOLATE MOUSSE
MAGIC IDEAS

Chocolate mousse can become so many things: a molten hot soufflé, a brûlée, a parfait or terrine – and many fancy cakes are conjured up with chocolate mousse that is mixed and moulded and glazed. Here are some ideas to start you off. Just close your eyes and lick your spoon and see where your taste buds take you.

FLAVOURED CHOCOLATE MOUSSE These are ideas for flavours and ingredients that you can scatter over the top of the finished mousse or serve on the side:

Sweet and boozy chestnuts: Cut cooked chestnuts into small pieces. Mix them with icing sugar and rum or brandy to taste. Scatter them over the top of the mousse.

Sweet flaked almonds: Dust flaked almonds with icing sugar on a baking tray. Toast them at 190°C/Gas 5 for 5-6 minutes, until they are lightly caramelised. Sprinkle them over the mousse.

Currants soaked in sherry: This needs a little forward planning. Put enough currants for however many portions you are serving into a bowl and cover them totally with oloroso sherry. Leave them to sit for at least 12 hours and much longer if you like. Spoon the currants and sherry over the mousse just before serving.

INTERESTING THINGS TO SPRINKLE ON TOP OF CHOCOLATE MOUSSE
Try: Chunks of chocolate • Chopped red chilli • Salt flakes or fleur de sel • Brandy, rum or Grand Marnier • Balsamic syrup (this has to be thick syrup, not thin vinegar)

GOOD FRUIT TO SERVE ALONGSIDE CHOCOLATE MOUSSE

Bananas, cooked or raw, mixed with dulce de leche. Dried bananas are also good with chocolate mousse

Peeled orange segments, with Grand Marnier if you'd like it boozy

Raspberries

Poached or tinned pears, with Poire William if you'd like it boozy

CHOCOLATE MOUSSE WITH VANILLA CREAM I like to serve dark chocolate mousse with whipped cream or crème fraîche. The best version is double or whipping cream, lightly whipped then seasoned with the seeds from a vanilla pod and a touch of icing sugar.

CHOCOLATE ETON MESS Fold chocolate mousse together with vanilla whipped cream (see previous idea), just enough to marble it, broken-up meringues from the shop, a touch of your favourite booze and some broken-up praline or nutty chocolate (or, if you fancy it fruity, raspberries, orange segments, chopped pears or bananas).

SUPER-RETRO ART-DECO BRANDY BASKET Use a star nozzle to pipe chocolate mousse into a brandy-snap basket from the shop. Swirl a little whipped cream on top, decorate with glacé cherries, close your eyes and be transported back to the eighties.

CHOCOLATE MOUSSE BELLE HÉLÈNE Put a large spoonful of chocolate mousse onto your plate and place a poached or tinned pear on top. Serve with a scoop of vanilla ice cream on the side and, if you really want to go crazy, chocolate sauce.

CHOCOLATE BROWNIE Line a small deep tray with butter, grated chocolate and demerara sugar. Smooth a 4cm layer of the chocolate mousse over the top. Bake at 180°C/Gas 4 for 14–16 minutes then leave to cool slightly. You can make individual ones of these in cupcake wrappers too, then use some uncooked mousse for layering and icing.

CHOCO-PEAR BAKE Spread chocolate mousse over the top of hot or cold roasted, poached or tinned pears. Sprinkle the top with flaked almonds or sliced chestnuts, dust with icing sugar and bake at 180°C/Gas 4 for about 12–14 minutes until it just starts to soufflé around the edges.

CHOCOLATE MOUSSE CAKE The mousse can be spread in a 2cm layer across a re-usable non-stick mat on a baking sheet, and baked at 190°C/Gas 5 for 8–10 minutes until it is cake-like. Cool, then cut into rectangles and layer the baked mousse with some cold mousse. You could also add bananas, cooked pears, chestnut purée, dulce de leche, raspberries, praline or hazelnuts.

CHOCOLATE-STUFFED FRENCH TOAST Make a double-decker French toast with chocolate mousse in place of the lemon curd and jam inside, like Jake's French toast on p.216.

A NEW LOOK AT A CHOCOLATE CROISSANT Bake chocolate mousse in place of the almond cream inside and on top of a croissant, like the ultimate almond one on p.193.

Chocolate mousse & boozy prune brûlée

I once had access to an almost endless supply of mi-cuit plums - juicy, vanilla-scented beauties that were halfway between a plum and a prune. I haven't been able to get them for a while so I've developed ways to recreate their taste and texture. The prune flavour goes very well with all chocolate: softened with a little rum, they provide a boozy surprise beneath the mousse and echo the aroma of the caramelised demerara sugar on top. You can leave out the alcohol or pour a little into the adult portion(s) only if you're making this for kids as well. The eggs are raw so it's no good for pregnant women or tiny kids.

The ideal vessel for this is a wide, shallow dish that's 12.5cm wide and 3cm deep, as you get more surface to caramelise, but 140ml (average-sized) cups or ramekins will do.

Serves 2
Prep/cooking time 30 mins
Active time 20 mins

. . . .

40g demerara sugar, plus 2 heaped tbsp, for crisping the tops

6 tbsp water

½ vanilla pod

8 large soft prunes, de-stoned and cut into 5mm dice

1-2 tbsp rum or brandy (optional)

★ 180g chocolate mousse (p.232)

2-4 heaped tbsp crème fraîche

1. Start with the syrup for the prunes. Get a small (14cm) saucepan. Add the 40g demerara sugar and the water. Scrape the seeds out of the vanilla pod. Put the seeds and scraped pod into the pan. Bring to the boil. Add the diced prunes. Bring back to the boil. Lower the heat to low and simmer (be careful, there is very little liquid) for 3-4 minutes until the prunes have absorbed most of the syrup. Take the pan off the heat. Add the rum or brandy if you're using it.

2. Spoon the prunes and syrup over the bottoms of your dishes. Put them in the fridge for 5 minutes to cool them down. Boil your kettle.

3. Spoon the chocolate mousse over the top of the prunes. Fill a mug with boiling water. Dip a palette knife into the boiling water and smooth the top of the mousse. Ideally the mousse should be almost level with the top of the dish so you've got a little space for the sugar. Put the mousses in your fridge to stay set until you need them.

4. Sprinkle 1 tbsp demerara sugar over the top of each mousse. Wipe the sides of the dishes after you do, or the sugar will burn onto the rims and make the serving dishes hard to wash up.

5. Caramelise the sugar with a blowtorch, starting from about 10cm away to melt the sugar then moving closer to brown it.

6. Leave them for 2 minutes to let the sugar harden, then serve the crisp-topped mousses with the crème fraîche on the side.

Molten hot chocolate & dulce de leche mousse

This is a dessert for chocolate lovers, dessert lovers and food lovers in general. Cakey around the outside and melting in the middle, it is moreish beyond belief. The hot mousse makes an utterly delicious dessert for anyone on a wheat-free diet at Christmas time or at any time. If you don't have the shallow dishes that I suggest (in the photo) to cook the mousse in, you could use small pasta bowls, ramekins or ovenproof cups. You may need to adjust the cooking time by a minute or two if the mousse is deeper than 3-4cm.

This is a great assembly job for younger kids, and remember that 70% chocolate is better for them than any other 'chocolate' with very little cocoa and lots of sugar.

Serves 2

Prep/cooking time 20 mins

Active time 15 mins

. . . .

20g soft unsalted butter

2-3 heaped tbsp demerara sugar

4 heaped tbsp dulce de leche

★ 180g chocolate mousse (p.232)

2 balls vanilla ice cream

1 tbsp dried cranberries

Zest of 1 orange, taken off with a zester

Icing sugar, for dusting

2 tbsp brandy or rum (optional, and not for kids)

1. Preheat your oven to 180°C/Gas 4, rack position upper middle shelf. Boil your kettle.

2. Line 2 shallow dishes first with soft butter then with demerara sugar. Put them on a baking sheet.

3. Spoon 2 tbsp of dulce de leche into the middle of each dish. Spread the chocolate mousse over the top. Flatten it slightly with a palette knife or spoon dipped in boiling water.

4. Put your filled dishes on the baking sheet into the preheated oven and bake the mousses for 6-8 minutes. The tops and edges should be just set and the middles soft, wobbly and molten.

5. Scoop the ice cream into the middle of each mousse. Sprinkle the dried cranberries and orange zest over the top. Dust with icing sugar. Spoon over the brandy at your table.

Chocolate & chestnut purée Mont Blanc

This fairy tale of icing sugar snow-capped meringue mountains, dark chocolate mousse and lightly whipped cream is bewitching. The chocolate mousse is my lovely secret to make it richer and give it a bitter edge. With any dessert that has meringue, I have to add ice cream - they absolutely need each other. Ideally you need a piping bag with a star nozzle, but if you don't have one, don't worry, you can spoon everything on in slightly more rustic layers.

Kids (of any age) can become part of this story: pipe, dust, whip, make the mountain and just get carried away.

Serves 2

Prep/cooking time
20-25 mins

Active time 20-25 mins

. . . .

180-200g chestnut purée
(depends on size of
packet)

40g icing sugar, plus extra
for dusting

1 vanilla pod, split and
scraped

150ml double cream

140g chocolate mousse
(p.232)

2 balls vanilla ice cream

4 mini meringues
(all supermarkets do
a version of these)

1. I used tumbler-sized glasses for this, but just use what you have: small jars are fun, as are martini glasses.

2. Start with the chestnut cream. Set up your food processor. Add the chestnut purée, the 40g of icing sugar and the seeds from half the vanilla pod. Blend together for 2 minutes: this makes the purée lighter as well as combining the ingredients.

3. Get a medium-sized bowl. Add the cream and the rest of the vanilla seeds. Whip the vanilla cream to soft peaks.

4. A piping bag makes filling the glasses much easier, so if you have one, use it. Spoon the chocolate mousse into the bottom of 2 (or 3) glasses. Pipe the chestnut cream on top, followed by the whipped cream. You can prepare them in advance up to this point.

5. When you are ready to serve, top each with a ball of ice cream, 2 meringues, and a good snowy dusting of icing sugar.

Upside-down chocolate, banana & maple syrup tarts

Over 20 years ago, when I worked at the late Jean and Christophe Crotet's 2-star Michelin restaurant, L'Hostellerie de Levernois in Burgundy, we made chocolate puff pastry for a multi-layered version of this. I've wanted to recreate the glazed chocolate pastry ever since. Rather than making puff from scratch, the best way I've found for home cooks is to transform plain filo into chocolate pastry with a mixture of butter, icing sugar and cocoa. To have the chocolate 'tart top' in your repertoire gives you a great many options, as anything that goes with chocolate, from ice cream to pears to caramel, can go underneath to give you a speedy show-stopper.

Serves 2
Prep/cooking time 30 mins
Active time 25 mins

....

3 tbsp icing sugar

25g unsalted butter

1 tbsp cocoa powder

1 sheet filo pastry

100ml double cream

4 tbsp maple syrup

1 large banana

★ 100g chocolate mousse
(p.232)

Grated zest of ½ orange

1. Preheat your oven to 175-180°C/Gas 3-4, rack position upper middle shelf. Line a baking sheet with a re-usable non-stick mat. Put a cooling rack next to your cooker.

2. First make the sweet cocoa butter. Get a medium-sized bowl (or small pan). Sieve the icing sugar into it. Add the butter. Melt the butter and sugar in your microwave (or in the small pan on your cooker). Sieve the cocoa powder over the top. Stir the mixture until it is completely smooth.

3. Lay the filo sheet flat on your chopping board. Cut it in half lengthways. Brush half of it with a third of the sweet cocoa butter. Put the second half of the filo pastry on top. Press down well and press out any air bubbles. Brush the top of the pastry with the rest of the cocoa butter. (If the butter becomes hard to spread, warm it slightly and don't worry if it becomes a little clumpy, it'll be fine once it's baked.) Cut out 2 x 20cm long by 6cm wide rectangles. Put these onto your lined baking sheet. Bake the trimmings too, they're great as biscuits.

4. Bake the pastry for 5-6 minutes in your preheated oven until it is glazed and deep brown. Make sure you set a timer, as these burn very quickly. (If your oven has a hot spot at the back you'll need to turn them halfway through.) Use a palette knife to transfer the pastry to the cooling rack while it is still warm so that it doesn't stick.

5. Get a medium-sized bowl. Pour in the cream. Whip it to soft peaks. Add 2 tbsp of the maple syrup. Whip it to slightly firmer soft peaks.

6. Boil your kettle. Fill a mug with boiling water. Peel the banana then cut it half lengthways. Cut each half in half again. Put 2 lengths of sliced banana flat on each plate. Use an ice cream scoop dipped in boiling water to alternate 2 scoops of the cream and mousse on top of each portion of bananas. Trickle 1 tbsp maple syrup over the mousse and cream on each plate. Zest the orange over the top. Put a pastry rectangle on top of each.

SPONGE CAKE

This light, buttery and beautiful sponge is inspired by Delia Smith's recipe. I have tried many sponge techniques, from the highly technical egg-yolks-whisked-over-warm-water Genoise to a delicate egg-white meringue biscuit à la cuillère, but Delia's put-everything-in-together-and-mix method came out on top. I bake it in a thin rectangular baking tray so that it is easier to use for the different recipes that follow, and has no waste. Casey's super strawberry cake apart, you can use any shape of trimming to make the recipes.

I'll give you a cream cake, but it's time to look at sponge differently too, in place of bread in pudding and in place of a pastry base in a tartlet.

Making this cake is a perfect confidence-builder for kids because everything goes into the bowl together and gets well mixed, and it always comes out beautifully.

Makes 1 x 40 x 36 x 3cm rectangle (the typical size of tray that comes with a 60cm oven)

Storage Fridge at least 1 week. Freezer 3 months

Prep/cooking time 30-35 mins

Active time 15-20 mins

. . . .

350g self-raising flour

2 heaped tsp baking powder

6 large eggs

1 tsp vanilla extract

350g caster sugar

350g very soft unsalted butter

6 tbsp icing sugar

1. Preheat your oven to 180°C/Gas 4, rack position middle shelf. Line a 40 x 36 x 3cm baking tray with a re-usable non-stick mat. Put a cooling rack next to your cooker.

2. This is easiest made in an electric mixer. If you don't have one you can use an electric hand whisk.

3. Get a large mixing bowl. Sieve in the flour and baking powder. Add the large eggs, vanilla extract, caster sugar and soft butter. Whisk for about 5 minutes until the mixture is smooth and very well combined.

4. Spread the sponge mixture into a rectangle almost to the edges of the lined tray. The batter will be about 1.5cm thick, don't worry if it is a little uneven on top.

5. Dust the cake batter with the icing sugar. Bake it in your preheated oven for 14-16 minutes until it is golden. To test if the sponge is cooked or not, dip a skewer into the thickest part, it should come out dry.

6. As soon as the sponge is cooked, take it out of the oven and transfer to your cooling rack. Once it is cool, put a second rack or tray gently on top. Flip the sponge over. Peel off the re-usable non-stick mat.

How to store

Once the sponge is cool, cut it into sizes for the recipes that you want to make. For instance, 2 x 12cm circles for Casey's cake, 2 x 8cm circles for the citrus cake, 3 rectangles for the tiramisu, then 200g of trimmings for the pudding.

Clingfilm and label the sponge portions then freeze and/or refrigerate them. If the sponge has been in the fridge for a while and you want to freshen it up, you can do so in your microwave, on low. It is also wonderful toasted.

SPONGE CAKE
MAGIC IDEAS

Sponge is a great thing to have handy. It can be the base for trifle, tiramisu and even toast. You can change its character by soaking it with booze or spreading it with jam. Once the sponge has been in the freezer, the texture becomes firmer, but I've discovered that it freshens up beautifully in the toaster, oven or microwave.

Always keep whatever bits and bobs you end up with. However small or misshapen the trimmings, they are never too small or gnarly to make trifle and any other dessert that you are going to soak or shape into a mould.

LAYERED CHEESECAKE Line a loaf tin with clingfilm. Cut 3 slices of sponge to fit the tin. Soak them with jam, marmalade or booze (limoncello would be nice). In a bowl mix cream cheese with lemon zest, juice and icing sugar to taste. Crush some ginger biscuits. Layer sponge, crushed biscuits and cream cheese mix, finishing with sponge. Press the cake a little then cover with clingfilm and leave to set in the fridge for 6–8 hours. Serve in slices with citrus segments.

ROAST PINEAPPLE AND PASSIONFRUIT CAKE Peel a pineapple then cut it into 2cm thick slices, 1 per person. Smear each slice with butter and sugar or honey and roast at 220°C/ Gas 7 for 12–15 minutes until it is well caramelised. Cut 1 circle of sponge per person to the same size as the pineapple. Soak the sponge with hot marmalade and lemon juice, with booze or with sugar syrup. Put the roast pineapple onto the sponge circle. Scoop passionfruit pulp over the top. This is nice with vanilla ice cream or whipped cream mixed with Malibu or, if you've got some, lemon curd (p.208) mixed with passionfruit.

BAKED ALASKA This is complete madness and great fun, and you will need your blowtorch. Make a good-sized space in your freezer. Make a meringue mixture (you'll need to use an Italian meringue for this). Cut 3 sponge circles in ever-decreasing sizes. Douse these with your favourite booze. Use a hot scoop to pile scoops of whatever ice cream you fancy over each sponge circle. Put the medium circle on top of the large one, and the smallest one on top to make a pyramid. Leave a 2cm border around the sides. Pipe the meringue all over the ice cream, making sure that there are no gaps. You can now freeze the baked Alaska until you need it. Dust with icing sugar and then blowtorch the exterior until it is golden-brown all over.

MAGIC AFTERNOON-CUP-OF-TEA CAKES

Cut circles, triangles, rectangles or squares of cake. Toast them or warm them through for 3-4 minutes in your oven at 180°C/Gas 4. Here, if you don't have the jam or lemon curd in your Magic Fridge, you can easily buy it. Good things to put on top include: Raspberry jam (p.220) and clotted cream • Lemon curd (p.208) and citrus segments • Lemon curd mixed with passionfruit, with more passionfruit pulp on top • Lemon curd with berries or berry jam • Crème pâtissière (p.196) with marmalade • Crème pâtissière with blackberry jam (p.220) and fresh figs • Crème pâtissière (diplomat, p.200) mixed with chopped dried cranberries or apricots • Crème pâtissière (diplomat) with cocoa mixed in and grated chocolate on top (if you want to really go for it, melt some chocolate over this too) • Chestnut purée mixed with icing sugar, cream and grated chocolate • Dulce de leche and bananas • Cream and strawberries.

INTER-MAGICAL JAM WITH RASPBERRY JAM TRIFLE

By this stage, if you have got all of the sweet chapters together in your Magic Fridge and Freezer, you can magic them together into a dessert. Soak some sponge with your favourite booze, then layer it in a glass with fresh berries, jam (p.220), crème pâtissière (diplomat, p.200) and lemon curd (p.208).

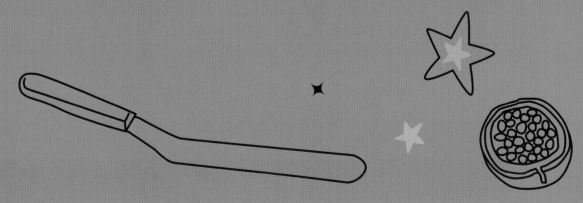

Citrus & passionfruit tartlet

This is a fresh and feisty dessert, very simple to prepare and a great way to make the most of your sponge cake, which just loves soaking up the sticky citrus juices. For a quicker, more rustic version, put the sponge onto your plates, spoon the sauce and segments over the top then dollop some cream into the middle. Or layer everything in a glass to transform the tartlet into a trifle.

This is a great one for the kids to help layer up, like building an upside-down house with the foundation on top.

Serves 2

Prep/cooking time 30 mins, plus 30 mins freezing

Active time 30 mins

- -

2 oranges

1 red grapefruit

Pulp and seeds of 2 passionfruit

100ml orange juice

75g caster sugar

100g chunky orange marmalade, plus 60g

125g mascarpone cheese

★ 2 x 8cm circles sponge cake (p.244), or you can squash trimmings together to make these

1. Get a medium-sized (20cm) saucepan. Remove the zest from one of the oranges into it with a zester. Peel the oranges and grapefruit with a sharp knife. Put a sieve over your saucepan. Hold one citrus fruit at a time over the sieve then cut out each segment of flesh between the white membranes. Squeeze the juice from the empty citrus membranes into the pan through the sieve. Transfer the citrus segments from the sieve into a bowl.

2. Add the passionfruit pulp, orange juice and sugar to the juice and zest in the saucepan. Bring to the boil over a high heat and reduce by two-thirds until the mixture is thick and sticky. (Watch the sauce as it can boil over.) Whisk in the 100g marmalade. Leave to cool. The sauce will become firm and jelly-like as it cools. Don't worry, this is how it should be. When the sauce is cool, add the orange and grapefruit segments.

3. Get a medium-sized bowl. Add the mascarpone cheese and the 60g marmalade. Whisk together.

4. Next, assemble the tartlets. Line a small tray or large plate with greaseproof paper. Put 2 x 8cm pastry rings on top, or use 2 x 8cm ramekins lined with clingfilm.

5. Put 2 grapefruit segments in the middle of each ring or ramekin. Surround the grapefruit with 4–5 orange segments. Add 1 tbsp sauce to each ring. Leave the rest of the segments in the remaining sauce. Smooth the mascarpone mixture over the top of the citrus and sauce, filling the pastry rings almost to the top. Freeze for 30 minutes (or refrigerate for 3–4 hours if you have time).

6. Put the cake circles on top of each ring or ramekin.

7. Warm the sauce just enough to liquify it. Spoon it and the citrus segments onto your plates.

8. Put a tray or large plate over the top of the tartlets. Turn them over so that the cake circles are on the bottom. Gently peel off the greaseproof paper. Warm the outsides of the pastry rings or ramekins and lift them off. (Remove the clingfilm if you're using the ramekins.) Put the little tartlets on top of the sauce. Serve.

Chestnut tiramisu

This sweet, rich, creamy, boozy and chunky cake is inspired by tiramisu and the Christmas chestnuts in Provence. You can make a speedy version that you can serve immediately by layering it all up in glass bowls. You will need a 23cm (or close to) loaf tin to make this.

This dessert must have the booze so is not one for kids!

Serves 8

Prep/cooking time 30 mins, plus 1 hour chilling

Active time 30 mins

....

 3 x 19 x 8cm rectangles sponge cake (p.244), or you can squash trimmings together to make this

400ml very strong coffee (as strong as you can make it)

5 tbsp dark rum, plus 2 tbsp

100g icing sugar, plus 75g, plus 60g

180-200g (depending on packet size) cooked chestnuts, chopped into tiny (5mm) dice

180-200g (depending on packet size) chestnut purée

250g mascarpone cheese

100g 70% cocoa chocolate, grated

1. Start with the sponge rectangles. Put them into a shallow tray just large enough to hold them. If you are using trimmings, piece them together to make roughly the size of the rectangles. They'll be a little messy to put into the loaf tin, but the end result is pretty much the same.

2. Get a medium-sized bowl. Add the strong coffee, the 5 tbsp rum and the 100g icing sugar. Mix together. Spoon this over the sponge rectangles, soaking them well. Leave the sponge to sit while you prepare the rest.

3. Get a medium-sized bowl. Add the chopped chestnuts, 2 tbsp rum and the 75g icing sugar. Toss well then leave to macerate for 10 minutes.

4. Get a medium-sized bowl. Add the chestnut purée and the 60g icing sugar. Whisk together vigorously for a couple of minutes to lighten the mixture. Put the bowl next to the sponge.

5. Strain the macerated chestnuts through a sieve over the top of the sponge to soak it a little more. Put the chestnuts back into their bowl. Add the mascarpone and grated chocolate. Fold together.

6. Brush the inside of your loaf tin with a little water to help the clingfilm stick. Line the tin with a double layer of clingfilm, leaving plenty overlapping the sides. Boil your kettle.

7. Use a large fish slice to put one of the soaked sponge rectangles along the bottom of the tin. Don't worry if it breaks a little, you can squash it back together. Scoop the chestnut purée mixture into the middle. Smooth it over the top with the fish slice dipped in hot water. Put a second sponge rectangle on top. Spread the mascarpone mixture over this. Put the final sponge rectangle onto the mascarpone. Press down gently.

8. Cover the top with the overlapping clingfilm. Press down lightly. Chill the tiramisu for at least an hour, or until you need it.

9. To serve, turn the tiramisu out of the loaf tin onto a chopping board. Lift off the clingfilm and slice it with a hot knife into 8 slices while it is still very cold.

Sponge & butter pudding with pear, white chocolate & ginger

This pudding is the most marvellous mischief. It is hot, rich and not too sweet. The juicy pear is kissed with caramel, soft sultanas, a ginger kick and creamy custard. (I've just been eating yesterday's from the fridge and it is also pretty good cold.)

Rather than bake the pudding too long I grill the top with a dusting of sugar to crisp it up. Serve with cold double cream. You will need a 20cm diameter ovenproof dish, 6cm deep.

There are lots of fun stages of this pud to get kids involved in. A particularly good one is when you pour the custard over and some of the sponge bubbles and burps and floats to the surface. My 11-year-old son Jake makes this for us at home now.

Serves 4-6 (there's no point in making less of this one, you'll eat it up pretty quickly)

Prep/cooking time 45-50 mins

Active time 15-20 mins

. . . .

350ml full-fat milk

150ml double cream

1 tbsp grated fresh root ginger

150g white chocolate, broken into small chunks

2 large eggs

3 large egg yolks

★ 20 x 20cm sponge cake (p.244), or roughly 200g trimmings

40g soft unsalted butter

100g raisins or sultanas

1 x 400g tin pear halves, drained and cut into quarters

30g demerara sugar

1. Preheat your oven to 190°C/Gas 5, rack position middle shelf.

2. Get a medium-sized (20cm) pan. Add the milk, cream and ginger. Bring to the boil, but watch carefully as it'll make an awful mess if it boils over. Add the white chocolate. Stir until it has melted.

3. Get a large bowl. Add the eggs and egg yolks and whisk together. Slowly pour over the hot milk mixture, whisking constantly until it is well combined.

4. Spread the butter over the sponge. If it is the trimmings you are using, just sort of dab the butter on and do the best you can. Put the sponge across the bottom of your ovenproof dish. Sprinkle the raisins or sultanas over the top.

5. Arrange the quartered pears over the top. Pour the custard over everything.

6. Bake in your preheated oven for 25-30 minutes until the custard is just set.

7. Sprinkle the top with the demerara sugar and caramelise it with your blowtorch. Alternatively, heat your grill and grill for 3-4 minutes until golden and crisp. (Grills vary enormously so do keep checking: it could be as quick as 2 minutes or as long as 5.) Serve hot.

Casey's super strawberry cake

My god-daughter Casey's favourite fruit is strawberries and I've made her a version of this cake for many years. She even ate the one in the photo! I make a bigger cake for Casey, of course, but I really liked the idea of giving a recipe for two people. I hope you don't mind, Casey, but I think couples are overlooked when it comes to cakes. Don't worry though, there will still be a bit leftover...

Make sure the sponge gets well covered with jam so it stays good and moist.

Serves 2, but can easily grow
Prep/cooking time 25 mins
Active time 25 mins

. . . .

For the mascarpone filling

250g mascarpone cheese

50g icing sugar

Seeds from 1 vanilla pod

250ml double cream

 2 x 12cm circles sponge cake (p.244)

150g strawberry or raspberry jam (p.220)

350g small strawberries, hulled

As many candles as you need or want

1. Start with the filling. Get a large bowl. Add the mascarpone, icing sugar and vanilla seeds. Whisk it all together until there are no lumps. Add the cream. Whisk together to firm peaks. Put this vanilla mascarpone into a piping bag with a star nozzle if you have one. If not, just do a slightly more 'rustic' version using a spoon.

2. If you are using sponge from the freezer or fridge, microwave it on low for a minute or two to freshen it up.

3. Spread the jam all over one side of each sponge circle.

4. Alternate the strawberries, with their noses facing outwards on the first sponge and upwards on the second, with strawberry-sized cream squirts. Once you have covered both sponge circles, put the one with the strawberry noses facing up on top of the other.

5. Put the candles in, light them, blow them out, make a wish, then do everything you can to make it come true.

MAGIC TRICKS TO HAVE UP YOUR SLEEVE

During the fifteen years *The Magic Fridge* has been in my mind and kitchen, it has evolved into a book with the clear goal to help people eat good food at home and enjoy cooking more. I tested and refined more than 100 recipes for this book, recording everything I did and used as a habit, as well as specifically for each dish. The more I did this, the more I recognised that there are key techniques I employ, and tools I rely on again and again, because they have become extensions of my body and mind from thirty years of cooking every day.

The most important techniques and tools in any kitchen are your senses: use them as often as you can while you cook. The more you get used to how food looks, smells, tastes and feels as it cooks and changes, the more confident you become. You refer to your instincts alongside the recipes, and the process starts to feel more natural as you enjoy each aroma, texture and the evolution of taste – you're not just waiting for the end result but enjoying how you get there.

It's also a great help to learn to cut, chop and slice well, whether you take a class or learn online. Chopping like a chef will make your time in the kitchen easier and more enjoyable.

Some of the specific techniques and ideas that follow are new discoveries; others I've adapted from restaurant tricks to use at home.

Magic Fridge 'braising'

To 'braise' is to cook ingredients in a smallish amount of liquid, with the goal of a great flavour exchange between the liquid, the main ingredient and the seasonings. Then by the time your dish is cooked you've created a sauce that harmonises the tastes of everything. I prefer braising to poaching, where the ingredient is completely submerged, and you lose flavour in the cooking liquid, which you generally don't use afterwards.

Braising is traditionally used to slowly cook large cuts of meat, but the three quicker methods I've developed here are for chicken legs and seafood that can be used for single portions upwards. These braising techniques are perfect for The Magic Fridge because they are one-pan meals that can be varied almost endlessly and flavoured or finished with the base recipes like basil pistou (p.28), red curry paste (p.76) or lemon butter (p.64).

Roast'n'braise chicken legs: I invented this to get the flavours of roast and braised chicken into a single technique. I fill an ovenproof pan with sliced or diced vegetables and/or cooked grains and pulses, stock and seasoning, cover these tightly with foil then put raw chicken legs, with the same seasonings, on top of the foil. I then put the pan in the oven where the chicken legs roast in the dry heat on top of the foil and the vegetables braise in the wet heat underneath.

Near the end, when the chicken skin is golden and surrounded with roasting juices, I take away the foil so that the chicken sits, still skin-side up, for the final ten minutes on top of the vegetables/grains that you've braised underneath. You finish with the best of both techniques: roast chicken skin and soft braised vegetables, all in the same single pan. (See pp.72, 104 and 116.)

Boil'n'braise seafood stew: I use this technique most often for recipes that are based on mussels, to cook the seafood and create a soup, broth or sauce in the same pan. As with a traditional bouillabaisse, you bring everything to the boil (*bouillir*) and then you lower the heat (*baisser*), at which point the ingredients braise in the cooking juices and start to add their own liquids and flavour.

Boil'n'braise is brilliant for one-pot dishes, because you can add potatoes, grains or pulses which can take on the taste of a small amount of seafood and stretch it into a feast, like the red curry on p.82.

Braised fish fillets: I learnt this glorious way to intensify a fish's flavour while keeping it as healthy as possible from the genius Raymond Blanc. Braising fish fillets doesn't need to involve any oil or fat, and rather than lose the flavours or have any of the hassle that comes with poaching or steaming, braising fish enhances its flavour.

You start with thinly sliced vegetables, sometimes cooked grains or pulses, and seasoning in an ovenproof pan. Soften them on your cooker, add wine, stock or water, then put your fish on top to gently braise in the oven. While the fillet braises, it develops a firm but moist texture and adds flavour to the liquid and vegetables below.

Once the fish is cooked, you can eat it, the vegetables and cooking liquor as is, or enhance the liquid with a Magic Fridge base recipe, like I did with the pistou for the sea bream on p.34 or the baked beans for the halibut on p.108.

Seasoned salts

Salt flakes and fleur de sel are great luxuries for me, a finishing touch for everything from sliced tomatoes to grilled meat. I like the salt's crunch on its own, or to add extra excitement, briefly mixed in a pestle and mortar with one or more of the following: cracked black pepper, dried thyme, dried savory, citrus zest, fennel seeds, herbes de Provence, or chopped dry or fresh chilli.

Coleslaws

Highly seasoned grated, sliced, ribboned or julienned vegetables make an excellent side dish. You get taste, crunch, freshness, variety, and often great beauty. On their own or mixed, you can make coleslaw with radishes, carrots, fennel, spring onions, mouli, celeriac, swede, turnip, cauliflower, or raw or cooked beetroot. Dress them with vinegar or lemon, then herbs or mustard. They don't have to be creamy or oily, but you can add mayonnaise, yoghurt or oil. You can also dress them with basil pistou (p.28), red curry paste (p.76) or salsa verde (p.52).

Lettuce 'bruschetta' (breadless open sandwich)

This is such a fun idea, and always so pretty. Depending on the size of 'sandwich' you want, use halved romaine, baby gem, chicory or endive where you'd usually use a slice of bread. You can rub the lettuce with garlic and douse it with olive oil as you would bread, then put anything from cheese and tomato to coronation chicken on top.

Vegetable 'steaks'

I call them steaks to help give the idea context, but why not serve a beautifully cooked pan- or oven-roasted carrot, swede, parsnip, beetroot or half aubergine as the focus of a dish? I've seasoned aubergines with just about everything possible and have now moved my focus to root vegetables. See recipes on pp.58, 90 and 91.

Mixing dried and fresh fruit

Using dried fruit as a seasoning for fresh fruit can greatly intensify the flavour of both. Try, for example, mixing fresh tomatoes with finely chopped dried tomatoes, or fresh fruit like apricots with dried apricots. This works for raw salads and cooked preparations like sauces and purées. See recipes on pp.84 and 199.

'Upside-down' tarts

These are sweet and savoury tarts that are built 'upside down' (see pp.146, 206, 218, 223 and 242). You crunch through the 'pastry' that you put on top at the last minute, into the 'cream' and then carve into the 'fruit'. The first time I worked on one was decades ago at Le Manoir, when I layered fresh porcini risotto with Parmesan crisps. The crisps with the risotto above and below became too soft too quickly so we ended up just putting one on top. A recent visit to Daniel Patterson's restaurant in San Francisco revived the idea for me. Putting the pastry on top saves you lining a tin, stops the pastry from going soft and means you can easily make tarts from one portion upwards.

Flavoured filo pastry

You can transform filo pastry into pepper pastry, chocolate pastry or citrus pastry by mixing the fat that you'd usually use to brush it with pepper chutney, icing sugar and cocoa powder or citrus zest. This, combined with the technique for upside-down tarts and flavoured creams, opens almost endless possibilities for your own tarts with the pastry on top. See pp.67, 146, 200, 218 and 242.

Flavoured creams

This was a standby as my 'mousse from the fridge' when I used to do the television programme *Ready Steady Cook*. It's the most delicious accompaniment to almost any dessert. The original version was 250ml double cream, 40g icing sugar and the seeds of half a vanilla pod whipped together. Instead of vanilla you can add ginger, citrus zest, maple syrup, golden syrup or elderflower cordial. If you want a cream that stays firm for longer, to layer a cake for example, use a mixture of half mascarpone and half cream.

Spiced Sugars

For raw or roasted fruit, using sugar is like using salt in savoury food: it's there to enhance the taste. At its simplest you can gently toss berries with caster sugar, leave them for 5 minutes to macerate and they become more intensely flavoured. Moving one step further, you can try using a mortar and pestle to grind herbs and/or citrus zest into granulated sugar. I use 4–6g citrus zest, mint or basil leaves to 40g sugar.

EQUIPMENT

There is equipment I use again and again: re-usable non-stick mats, a good non-stick pan, ovenproof pans, crème brûlée dishes. These are not random gadgets, but tools that make a difference. It starts with your hands and a sharp knife, because both can save you years of frustration over a lifetime making meals. The key thing is to have the right sized equipment for the right job and the number of people you cook for most often. Try and stick to the minimum that you need so that you have as little clutter as possible.

★ **Your hands** Work with two hands. Put things down on your work surface and free up both of your hands. Think of everything like a bag: if you hold a bag with one hand and try to get something out, it's much harder than if you put the bag down on a table then have two hands free. Analyse one normal session in your kitchen and you will see what I mean.

★ **Sharp knives** If you work with blunt knives you will make life much harder for yourself, you will have less fun and you are more at risk of a painful cut. Taking a cutting and sharpening course is a good idea too.

★ **A flat chopping board** and something to stop it slipping.

★ **Dishwasher** The most important piece of kit, not only to save you washing up, but to stack into as you go, to keep you tidy and organized so you can have more fun. Go for one with a quick cycle.

★ **Timer/Thermometer** I bought an inexpensive one that has a timer and a probe. You can set the alarm to tell you when the meat you are probing gets to the right temperature and you can put the probe in the oven to use it as an oven thermometer. I attach it to the shelf with a little clip. All ovens vary so get to know yours and be sure to keep an eye on what you're cooking.

★ **Non-stick baking mat** Get the thick, more expensive ones, nothing sticks to these. They make it so much easier to transfer tarts and pastry to cooling racks and you can re-use them again and again.

★ **Microwave** A microwave is the best thing to reheat in and to melt or soften butter and chocolate.

★ **Large kettle** Much faster than a pot on the cooker to boil water. Also great for filling your sink without wasting lots of water waiting for it to get hot.

★ **Shallow pan** A medium/large (24–30cm) ovenproof shallow pan that you have a tight fitting lid for. This is what I use most often, for boiling green vegetables, mussels, boil'n'braise and roast'n'braise.

★ **Non-stick pans** A heavy-bottomed 20cm non-stick pan for pancakes. A heavy-bottomed 24–30cm non-stick pan for frying fish with its skin on. Buy good ones in the first place, use a heatproof plastic spatula and wipe rather than wash the non-stick surface; never touch it with anything abrasive. Store them with kitchen paper protecting the non-stick surface and these should last you for a lifetime. These pans should be able to go straight from hob to oven so that there is no change in their temperature that'd you'd get from transferring your ingredients to a tray, and you save on washing up later.

★ **Cooling rack** A small cooling rack that fits over the top of a plate or small tray to rest meat on and transfer baked pastry onto.

★ **Electric scales and spare batteries** So you can weigh directly into the pan or bowl you are going to work in.

★ **Measuring spoons** These are a much more efficient way of measuring small quantities than a measuring jug.

★ **Piping bag** Not so much to decorate with but to fill dessert glasses with cream and cream mixtures. It makes life so much easier. To fill a piping bag on your own, put a peg on the piping end, open the bag over a jar or measuring jug, then you have two hands to fill it with.

★ **Blowtorch** Having a good blowtorch opens up the possibility to make a multitude of quick and delicious desserts.

★ **Mandolin** One of these means that you can quickly cut gorgeous ribbons of carrot, beetroot, courgette, cucumber and circles of radish to light up your salads. You can also cut the strips of vegetables known as julienne. Make sure you keep the safety guard; good mandolins are incredibly sharp.

★ **Heatproof spatula** Vital for getting every last drop of gravy or sauce out of pans and bowls.

★ **Heatproof brush** To glaze ingredients as they cook, and to make sure that you serve meat and fish glistening with their flavoursome cooking juices.

★ **Tongs and large tweezers** Both are the most practical way to extend your hands into hot and oily ingredients. Tongs for large, tweezers for small.

★ **Fish slice** A wide, long, sturdy, non-flexible one makes transferring and turning large hot ingredients much easier.

★ **A big serving spoon** To make light work of dishing up at the table.

★ **Mortar and pestle** To make the spiced sugars and salts.

★ **Storage containers** On the whole I use a mixture of jars and plastic containers with lids that I upcycle. For plastic, I would recommend square or rectangular containers that stack well in the fridge or freezer. Airtight is ideal, but you can always use clingfilm to help.

★ **Glass bowls** Making layered desserts in glasses or glass bowls makes life easier because you don't have to plate them up later. It also means that because, like the panna cotta with raspberry jam on page 228, you don't have to turn them out, they can be more gently set so that they melt rather than bounce in your mouth.

★ **Crème brûlée dishes** These flat gratin dishes with two small ears, like the ones on p.204, open up a world of possibility for crème brûlées and gratins. The reason these dishes are better than ramekins is that you want a good amount of surface to caramelise. The size I use is approx. 12cm across the top and 3cm deep.

★ **Shallow bowl for salads** Salads are best dressed in shallow bowls or dishes so that you don't bruise the salads and that everything gets evenly seasoned. Ideally, always buy dishes that can go straight from the kitchen to the table.

STOCKING YOUR KITCHEN

These are ingredients that I generally have on hand:

In the fridge

- Dulce de leche
- Vac-pac beetroot
- Onion or tomato chutney
- Sunblush or semidried tomatoes in oil
- Roquito pepper pearls
- Stock and concentrated stock
- Jam
- Bottled smoothies for coulis and fruit soup. Can also be used to make sorbet
- Crème fraîche
- Mozzarella cheese
- Mascarpone cheese
- Block of Parmesan cheese
- Miso paste

In the freezer

- Filo pastry
- Feuille de brick (When you buy this, unwrap it and freeze it in the number of sheets that you are most likely to use. This way, you don't dry out all of the pastry when you only want to use a couple of sheets.)
- Puff pastry sheets
- Frozen berries
- Ice cream
- Frozen stock
- Peas
- Broad beans
- Soya beans (edamame)

In the spice drawer

- Salt flakes
- Cayenne pepper
- Piment d'Espelette
- Curry powder
- Ras-el-hanout
- Paprika
- Smoked paprika
- Herbes de Provence
- Chinese 5-spice powder
- Turmeric

In the store cupboard

- Tinned chickpeas
- Tinned haricot beans
- Tinned pears, apricots
- Tinned chopped tomatoes
- Tubes of tomato purée
- Pouches of cooked grains: quinoa, freekeh, spelt, mixed grains, lentils
- Dried seaweed
- Dried porcini mushrooms
- 1-minute polenta
- Piquillo or other tinned peppers
- Chestnut purée
- Pouches of cooked chestnuts

- Vanilla pods
- Extra virgin olive oil
- Vegetable oil
- Balsamic syrup and vinegar
- Red and white wine vinegar
- Dried orange zest
- Bay leaves
- Meringue nests and minis
- Powdered stock or bouillon, or paste
- Black olives à la grecque (tins or jars)
- Home-made salad dressing

On the windowsill

Herbs keep and taste better, looked after, for longer in pots on the windowsill than they do if you buy packets to put in the fridge. You almost never need a whole bunch for a recipe and this way you always have them as fresh as possible. Keep the pots in a saucer, and water them from below.

- Basil
- Mint
- Chives
- Parsley

- Coriander
- Rosemary
- Thyme

This book begins and ends with the idea that cooking and eating can make you feel magical, but the way you get there is to be pragmatic and prepared. This last recipe is the culinary composition of what it all means – something so silly and beautiful, delicious and ridiculous, but thanks to the Magic Fridge, pretty easy to make.

To make this Kiwi pavlova in the shape of a French croquembouche I've taken meringue from the store cupboard, lemon curd, sponge and jam from the base recipes (p.208, p.244 and 220) and vanilla cream from the 'Magic Ideas' on p.234, and put them all together in great crazy, huge, fairy-tale dessert from this fantastic fridge of ours.

Pavlovabouche

Put a circle of sponge onto a large plate and spread berry jam across the top. Alternate blobs of lemon curd and strawberries around the outside. Top the sponge with 4 meringue nests them fill them with lemon curd. Fill the space left in the middle with vanilla whipped cream and strawberries. Stick 3 meringue nests on top. Fill them with curd. Fill the centre with vanilla cream and strawberries. Stick 1 meringue nest on top, fill it with lemon curd then pipe vanilla cream all around it. Put 6 large strawberries on top. Pipe cream on top of the strawberries. Top with 3 mini meringues. Put a blob of curd, then cream, then a final strawberry on top. Decorate any gaps on the outside with mini meringues and strawberries. Dust with icing sugar and serve with ice cream or sorbet.

Have a laugh with me and my pavlovabouche, then go to your kitchen and make your own Magic Fridge; every day, every time you cook, touch and taste a bit of wonder through the act of making meals. It's as simple as you want it to be: a piece of toast with pistou, a lovely pear with lemon curd, some creamy cheese and pepper chutney. Get prepared and you'll find magic all around you.

THE END
of the book.

THE BEGINNING
of your Magic Fridge.

Index

Acknowledgements

The Magic Fridge has been in my life for many years, but the book burst to life thanks to the vision and brilliance of Natalie Bellos (Maestro) my Commissioning Editor at Bloomsbury. Nat challenged me every step of the way and our constant back and forth, over years, each time yielding improvement and often new ideas was an exhilarating process. Thanks for loving *The Magic Fridge* Maestro Nat, for believing in it and in me and thanks for your creativity and the openness of your magical mind. Thanks to Assistant Editor Lena Hall, a rising star, for your great attention to detail, professionalism and boundless enthusiasm. Thanks to my long-time friend and wonderful Copy Editor Susan Fleming for your patience, finesse, skill, expertise and encouragement.

Thank you Peter Knab for your eyes, artistry, brilliant work and the way you combine great experience with perpetual evolution in your photography. Also for your incredible hard work and dedication during the long shoot days and beyond. Thanks and love to Diana Knab for the opportunity to do Le Baou d'Infer Cookery School where *The Magic Fridge* began.

Thank you to the endlessly imaginative artists/designers Julyan Bayes and Brian Roberts at Us Now. Your drawings and designs are glorious, funny and clever, all the magic I dreamt of but couldn't visualise until I saw your wonderful work. Thanks to the superb prop stylist Lydia McPherson and assistant Lauren Miller for your wonderful creative choices, hard work and skill. Thanks to my brilliant assistants on the shoot Kelly Mauger (great work on the jam marbling), Ethan Flack (fantastic pancakes), Susanne Downes, Slavka Georgieva and Krasimira Videva. Thanks Ray Hussey for your help too.

At Bloomsbury thanks to Head of Digital Marketing Tram-Anh Doan, Senior Publicity Manager Ellen Williams, Marketing Manager Sarah Williams, Production Manager Marina Asenjo and the wonderful Xa Shaw Stewart. Thanks to Kate Cubitt and her team at Bloomsbury Australia. Thanks to indexer Hilary Bird and proofreader Becci Woods for such care and attention.

Thanks to Alison Cowan for the great start and Lisa Pendreigh for seeing the project through. Thanks to the inspirational Richard Atkinson for the *Everybody Everyday* meeting I'll never forget which bought me into the Bloomsbury family that I am so proud to be part of. Thanks to my dear Ben Mason for the same meeting and for getting *The Magic Fridge* deal done. Thanks to Anna Power at Johnson & Alcock and Emily Hayward-Whitlock, Leigh Rodda and Kaye Freeman at The Artists Partnership, I look forward to the wonderful projects we have ahead.

Great thanks to three geniuses who have given me so much in so many different ways, Raymond Blanc, Delia Smith and Justin North.

Thanks to Clive Fretwell for teaching me so many techniques and how to run a cookery school. Thanks to the late Pierre Meyer and Mo Hall. To Mike and Pam Taylor, Grant Allen, Martin Bosley, Jean Bardet, the late Jean Crotet, Jean-Pierre Jacob, Rachel Priestley, Alick Shaw, Don Alfonso Iaccarino and my family, Dylan, Penn, Marian, Dad, Anna and Tomo for your influences and inspiration. Thanks to Casilda Grigg for commissioning a Magic Fridge article for the telegraph. Mary O'Hare for stocking the original magic Fridge with me, to Fiona Hamilton-Fairly at thekidscookeryschool.co.uk charity. Thanks to Charlie Mclean and Kirsten Blake for your support.

Huge thanks to Clive Moxham, Terence Faulkner, Sanjay Davda, Chris Waters, Mark Leatham and Oliver Leatham at Merchant Gourmet, it's wonderful to work with you guys and our wonderful ingredients and becomes ever more exciting with our future projects, thanks also to Caroline Moore. Thanks to Ken Watts for eggs, Johnny at Flying Fish, Martin and Charlie Mash for veg, Rachel and Geoff at Cornfield Bakery, Nicki and Jason at Cricks Butchers, and to Colin Ring for the lifts and laughter.

To finish with a bit of magic, it was Ray Latham, the milkman I worked for three decades ago who gave me the idea and contacts to start working with food. Thank you Ray, I found work I love because you exposed me to it, I wish everyone could be so lucky. My work now is to expose as many people as I can to the joy of cooking and eating together, along with all the good it can do.

Bloomsbury Publishing

An imprint of Bloomsbury Publishing Plc

50 Bedford Square	1385 Broadway
London	New York
WC1B 3DP	NY 10018
UK	USA

www.bloomsbury.com

British Library Cataloguing-in-Publication Data

A catalogue record for this book is available from the British Library.

Library of Congress Cataloguing-in-Publication data has been applied for.

ISBN: HB: 978-1-4088-6237-7

ePub: 978-1-4088-6371-8

2 4 6 8 10 9 7 5 3 1

Designer: Us Now, www.us-now.com
Photographer: Peter Knab
Illustration: Us Now, www.us-now.com
Copy editor: Susan Fleming
Prop stylist: Lydia McPherson
Indexer: Hilary Bird

Printed in China by RRD Asia Printing Solutions Limited
Bloomsbury Publishing Plc makes every effort to ensure that the papers used in the manufacture of our books
are natural, recyclable products made from wood grown in well-managed forests. Our manufacturing processes
conform to the environmental regulations of the country of origin.

To find out more about our authors and books visit www.bloomsbury.com. Here you will find extracts,
author interviews, details of forthcoming events and the option to sign up for our newsletters.